¶B The Practitioner's Bookshelf

Hands-On Literacy Books for Classroom Teachers and Administrators

Dorothy S. Strickland
FOUNDING EDITOR, LANGUAGE AND LITERACY SERIES

Celia Genishi and Donna E. Alvermann
LANGUAGE AND LITERACY SERIES EDITORS*

---

* For a list of current titles in the Language and Literacy Series, see *www.tcpress.com*

Literacy in the Welcoming Classroom

CREATING FAMILY–SCHOOL PARTNERSHIPS THAT SUPPORT STUDENT LEARNING

JoBeth Allen

Foreword by Katherine and Randy Bomer

Teachers College, Columbia University
New York and London

National Writing Project
Berkeley, CA

Published simultaneously by Teachers College Press, 1234 Amsterdam Avenue, New York, NY 10027, and the National Writing Project, 2105 Bancroft Way, Berkeley, CA 94720-1042

Copyright © 2010 by Teachers College, Columbia University

All rights reserved. No part of this publication may be reproduced or transmitted in any form or by any means, electronic or mechanical, including photocopy, or any information storage and retrieval system, without permission from the publisher.

The National Writing Project (NWP) is a professional development network of more than 200 university-based sites, serving teachers across disciplines and at all levels, early childhood through university. The NWP focuses the knowledge, expertise, and leadership of our nation's educators on sustained efforts to improve writing and learning for all learners.

Photographs courtesy of Monira Al-Haroun Silk, JoBeth Allen, and Jan Miller Burkins.

Grateful acknowledgment is made for permission to reproduce the following:

"The Old School House is Waiting," by Colton Lowder. From Plemmons, A. (2006). Capturing a community. *Schools: Studies in Education, 3*(1), 81–113. ©2006 by the University of Chicago Press.

Figure 5.1: Adapted with permission from *Engaging Families: Connecting Home and School Literacy Communities* by JoBeth Allen, Barbara Michalove, and Betty Shockley. Copyright © 1995 by JoBeth Allen, Barbara Michalove, and Betty Shockley. Published by Heinemann, Portsmouth, NH. All rights reserved.

Library of Congress Cataloging-in-Publication Data

Allen, JoBeth.
   Literacy in the welcoming classroom: creating family–school partnerships that support student learning / JoBeth Allen; foreword by Katherine and Randy Bomer.
      p. cm.
   Includes bibliographical references and index.
   ISBN 978-0-8077-5077-3 (pbk.)
   1. Language arts (Elementary) 2. Education, Elementary—Parent participation. 3. Home and school. I. Title.
   LB1576.A61287 2010
   372.6—dc22

2009049415

ISBN 978-0-8077-5077-3 (paper)
Printed on acid-free paper
Manufactured in the United States of America

17   16   15   14   13   12   11   10   8   7   6   5   4   3   2   1

Contents

Foreword

JoBETH ALLEN'S NEW BOOK is the one we educators most need for twenty-first-century schools. In showing how to create partnerships among schools, homes, and communities, this book will help school communities strengthen themselves in their most vulnerable, most overlooked areas. American schools are becoming more diverse than ever before. Immigrant children are the fastest growing segment of the U.S. population, and Latinos are the fastest growing ethnic group. It is increasingly likely that teachers are involved with children from households different from that of their upbringing, and as Allen points out, children from all ethnicities and socioeconomic circumstances may reside in families that have guardians, grandparents, same-sex couples, or single parents in charge of them. We are at the beginning of a new era in American education, one in which school teachers and administrators cannot know enough about the experiences, resources, and languages children bring to school without reorienting the school toward learning from children's homes and neighborhoods. Because there is more diversity, there is also more need for connection to families, more need of their knowledge and partnership, more need of listening to the people who know their children best. This book provides practical, actionable ways of beginning that work.

The relationships that the author wants us to create in schools have respect at their center. When a school places respect at the center of its relationships with families, the school allows itself vulnerability—the possibility of being affected by others, the possibility of changing even cherished ways. Jerry Harste once said that a person should enter into dialogue expecting one of the pillars of their own thinking to be knocked out from under them in that conversation. Only then would the person be truly inquiring. Schools that enter into dialogue with parents and guardians might find themselves considering their work in whole new ways.

That kind of dialogue, which Allen calls us into, is very different from approaching parents with "expectations" and "nonnegotiables." This isn't about getting families to do school at home; it's about bringing homes and neighborhoods into the language and literacy activities and learning inquiries in schools. This book shows us how to engender more respectful, caring, and engaged partnerships that result in both children and adults learning more. As Allen writes, "I think these would be great questions to write about at the beginning of monthly faculty and or grade level meetings: What have you learned from families this week? What difference has it made for your teaching/students' learning?" This question, if we all took it on, would change what school means for all our children.

In a time when pressure on schools often leaves educators looking for someone to blame, it is a gift to be reminded that families that lack income do not lack intelligence. People are not poor because of personal or familial inadequacies, but because of the distribution of wealth in our society. For schools to treat families in poverty as if there is something broken in their basic life capacities is more than disrespectful; it is subtractive, separating students from the resources they had before they came to school. This is one of the ways that the poor are made poorer. Allen calls for relationships around schooling that allow students to hold onto their cultural wealth, their family and community connections, their personal experience, and to use those resources in growth toward high expectations for academic success. Children are motivated and strengthened by having family and neighbors supporting them, rather than being taught as if there were something wrong with the people and places they come from.

This book is about people doing things together—about shared thinking, responsibility, and authority, about togetherness and community. A single teacher reading it alone will immediately start thinking of things to do with others, but one of the many strengths of this book are Allen's extensive roadmaps for colleagues, family, community members, and even students to read this book together and invent ways to live and learn from each other.

—*Katherine and Randy Bomer*

Acknowledgments

MY DEEPEST THANKS go to the outstanding teachers I learn with and from. Many of the teachers featured in this book are colleagues in the Red Clay Writing Project, which is very dear to my heart. Red Clay teachers who shared their insights here include Jennifer Beaty, Jennifer Ellis, Chris Hansen, Miriam McMillan, Andrea Neher, and Andy Plemmons. I count on spirited conversations about families and schools with thoughtful Red Clay colleagues Stephanie Jones and Jan Miller Burkins. Jan and Monira Silk shot the lovely photographs that give a face to family–school partnerships in each chapter.

Other educators who have opened their classrooms to me and my heart and mind to their students and families include my longtime collaborators Barbara Michalove and Betty (Shockley) Bisplinghoff, as well as teachers who participated in the PhOLKS (Photographs of Local Knowledge Sources) study group: Vinette Fabregas, Karen Hankins, Gregory Hull, Hattie Lawson, Steve Piazza, Cyndy Piha, Linda Sprague, Sybil Townsend, and Carmen Urdanivia-English. I appreciate the ongoing discussion of family–school partnerships with Family Engagement Specialist Mary Kelly and the teachers at Alps Road Elementary in Athens, Georgia. Teachers, parents, and administrators from across the country have shared memories, insights, and challenges when I've had the opportunity to visit their schools.

This book's Online Supplementary Materials for parents and caregivers on the Teachers College Press website are written in both English and Spanish. It is particularly fitting that the translation team for the Spanish version are a mother and daughter. Soria Colomer and her mother Betty Colomer, who lives in Honduras, spent many hours with the family's big blue Spanish-English dictionary when Soria was growing up. When Soria went to college, she and her mom collaborated via email on translation projects by drawing from their linguistic strengths—Betty's Spanish and Soria's English. It has been an empowering partnership for both, and a way for Betty to be actively involved in her daughter's postsecondary education.

And the Deepest Gratitude Award this year goes to—it's a tie between my husband of 40 years and my editor at Teachers College Press. Lew, I treasure our daily walks and lively discussions about our children and other people's children, about education and equity, about the world as it is and the world as it might become. Meg, you are more than an editor; you are a true collaborator, whose keen ear and knowledgeable suggestions have shaped this project from the beginning.

I am rich in family–school partnerships!

Family–School Literacy Partnerships

"SHE NEVER EVEN takes time to look through the Thursday folder," Alex sighed. He and Mary, the school's family engagement specialist, were driving to visit H.J's mother. "I really work hard on communicating with parents. Every week I send home all the children's work, notes to parents, and updates on what we are doing. But his mother doesn't seem to read them. There were so many papers crammed in H.J.'s backpack that I finally just threw everything away," Alex explained. "Thanks for coming with me on this home visit, Mary. His mom never did show up or even let me know she wasn't coming to parent–teacher conferences."

When they reached the apartment, Janisse graciously welcomed both teachers, apologizing for the darkness. There were no bulbs in the light sockets, no tables, no chairs. They sat on the lone piece of furniture, a brown sofa. Janisse explained that they had recently moved from out of state and that she had been looking for a job every day.

Then she asked, "How is H.J. doing with his school work?"

Alex responded, as he and Mary had discussed, "First, I'd like you to tell me about your son, and how you think he's doing."

Janisse beamed. "H.J. loves school, and especially you—he thinks you are a great teacher. He is so proud of the work he is doing! He brings it home in his backpack every Thursday, but he won't let me take anything out. I can look at them, but then I have to put them back in his folder, and he puts it right back in his backpack so he doesn't lose anything."

Janisse went on to explain that it was hard for her, raising three children on her own without any family in town. "The kids don't have anything to do in the evenings. We don't have a TV. I'm not sure how to help them with their homework—what do you think? How can I help H.J., especially with his reading?"

Alex, Janisse, and Mary brainstormed ways they could work together to support H.J.'s learning. Alex explained the kind of work they would be doing in the next few weeks, and said he'd talk with H.J. about sharing his Thursday folder a bit more freely. He explained that there were often "family homework" suggestions in the folders, ideas for things Janisse and H.J.—and even the other children—could do together related to what they were learning in class. Mary invited Janisse to come to the Family Resource Center to check out games that the whole family could enjoy in the evenings.

A partnership was born.

LIVING THIS BOOK AS A DIALOGUE

Family–School Literacy Partnerships is an invitation to you, educators and families, to enter into a dialogue. Elementary classroom, art, music, physical education, special education, and ESL teachers; media specialists and literacy coaches and instructional lead teachers; principals and paraprofessionals and noncertified staff who care deeply about the children in your school—welcome to this book. I invite parents, foster parents, grandparents, guardians, single-parent families, two-mom or two-dad families, whatever makes your family a family. Join in a dialogue with teachers and families from around the United States, adults who have collaborated to support, enhance, and expand the literacy learning of the children in their homes, their classroom, their care.

I'd like to think of this as a beach book: You know, one you really *want* to read instead of really *have* to read? Maybe you could start it at the beach, feel the syncopation of the waves of ideas with the ocean waves, muse about the possibilities as you sink your feet in the sand. But ultimately this is a book that is meant to be lived, not just read. And it cannot be lived in solitude—even that replenishing solitude of the ocean, or lake, or mountain retreat. It is meant to be lived by a community and to create that community, bringing together educators and families.

Dialogue as a Study Group

Literacy in the Welcoming Classroom is organized in nine chapters and designed for use by a study group or whole faculty. It's meant to be read over time, rather than in a single reading and one rushed discussion on the first day of preplanning. Haven't we been there all too often? "Teachers, we have a mandate to completely change the way we teach reading, the assessment instruments, the 27 reporting forms, and by the way, you'll need to incorporate these new instructional strategies in science and social studies too. Classes start Monday!"

Here are some saner possibilities:

- Make family–school partnerships the focus of whatever group at your school includes, or could include, parents or other family members, such as a Parent–Teacher Advisory Council. The group might read a chapter a week for 9 weeks or 9 months or whatever schedule fits your personal and professional lives.
- Discuss one chapter a month during faculty meetings. Some schools have faculty time set aside for professional

learning, some for meeting school and district improvement plans, and some meet once or twice a month for general faculty business. What if you set aside 30 minutes at one of these meetings, once a month, to discuss school–family literacy partnerships?

- Form a study group. Maybe not everyone in the school is interested, but where three or more are gathered—you have a study group. You might issue an open invitation: "Anyone who is interested in looking at ways we can form partnerships with families to support student learning meet in the library (or cafeteria, or a nearby coffee shop) Thursday afternoon after we get the kids on the bus." Those who come will determine the time, structure, and goals of the group. Schools where teachers issue this kind of "y'all come" invitation are usually ones where teacher leadership is valued and things get done.

- Form a study group for just your classroom. Invite all families. Maybe some of the kids will want to join in! Download materials (available in English and Spanish) from http://www.tcpress.com to share with parents. These are short versions of some of the processes in each chapter.

Start Anywhere, Anytime

So you like these possibilities *but* . . . it's December already, so should you wait until next year? No, just "dip in" wherever your school's needs and interests lie: Maybe you'll decide to explore family (home) visits (it's never too late in the year) or student-led conferences (you have another one in the spring, right?) or parent-teacher-student authored books. *But* . . . it's April and everyone is exhausted from being in the crosshairs during testing season, so isn't it really too late to do anything this year? Not so. If you are reading this book, you can propose several options for next year (study groups, grade-level meetings). People might even take on assignments over the summer—very small assignments—to read at the beach. Maybe you'll get volunteers to read one chapter each and be ready to talk about it when you start back in the fall. Maybe there are two or three parents who are interested, and they can talk to two or three more.

There are many ways to "live" this book. You might be seeking particular information and pull out a single chapter, such as Chapter 8 on student-led conferences. It's okay to read it out of order—

really. You don't even have to read the whole book. Paulo Freire's (1970) *Pedagogy of the Oppressed* is one of the most influential books I've ever read, and I reread parts of it regularly. In Chapters 1–3, I learn something new every time. The final chapter? Not so much.

In living the ideas in *Family–School Literacy Partnerships* we'll focus primarily on partnerships with families supporting student literacy learning at home. There are many excellent school-based practices that you can read about elsewhere (e.g., Allen, 2007; Henderson, Mapp, Johnson, & Davies, 2007). As we'll find out in the next chapter, research tells us that family involvement leads to increased student learning when it is focused on learning and invites interaction at home rather than requesting that parents come to school (Henderson & Mapp, 2002). Literacy partnerships with families at home have the potential to be more frequent than school events, more intimate adult-child time, more connected to the child's world, and in the more familiar language of the home.

The only conditions that are important—and they are crucial—are starting with a respect for families regardless of circumstances, the belief that families and teachers can work together to support student learning, a questioning mind-set toward what you are currently doing (and toward what you read in this book), and an openness to examining new ideas and refining the tried and true. The rest we can explore together.

DEAR READER CHAPTER STRUCTURE

Each chapter has four sections that move the reader from his or her local school, family, and community to the broader world of educational practice, then "back home" to plan specific actions. While the amount of space devoted to each varies with the topic, your will always have the DEAR reader structure. No, that's not Drop Everything And Read, although that's always a good idea. This DEAR is Discuss, Explore, Act, Read.

- *Discuss.* What's happening at your school, in your community, with your teachers, families, and students? It's so important to know where you are before you decide where you want to go.
- *Explore.* What have other families and teachers done in this area (e.g., home visits, conferences)? Individual teachers

and families have formed partnerships to support student learning in myriad ways. No program can be plucked from one school and successfully plopped down in a different school. On the other hand, teachers and families can learn from other teachers and families, and develop local practices that make sense for them.

- *Act.* What will you do together that will lead to increased student learning? You might make a connection, develop a strategy, evaluate current practices, adapt someone else's good idea. Put in the simplest terms, try something. You have figured out where you are, where you want to go, and what others have done. Where you start is not as important as starting somewhere. Create a continuous cycle of what Paulo Freire called praxis: action-reflection-action.

- *Read.* How can you read more about particular practices and the theories and research underlying them? This book provides the nitty-gritty, no-frills core principles and practices, enough to get you started in forming meaningful partnerships. As you discuss, explore, and act, you'll want to know more, to understand on a deeper level.

PICTURE A PARTNERSHIP FOR LEARNING

I have one small suggestion as you get started. Take pictures of some of your students and their families the next chance you get— the ice cream social, open house, a soccer game, drop-by visits to your classroom, a walk through the neighborhood with some of your students. Print these photos and display them where you are most likely to read and think about the ideas in this book: a family bulletin board in your classroom, by your reading chair at home, a wall in the library where you have faculty meetings. Keep the families with you, not families in general, but the families of Rodolpho and Sohail, of LaToya and Abdirizak and Brandon.

Picture *your* partnerships for literacy learning.

CHAPTER I

Partnerships to Foster Learning

WHAT DO TEACHERS "count" as parental involvement? What do parents count as their own involvement in the education of their children? Why don't families always know the answer to the first question or educators to the second?

Teachers at McCoy Elementary School in Kansas City, mostly White, were concerned that Latino parents were "not involved"— meaning they rarely came to school. Further, some children missed a great deal of school when families traveled to Mexico for extended periods. School staff invited families to focus group meetings on student learning, and both groups started to learn from each other.

- When they learned that trips to Mexico were a problem for their children, families agreed to go during vacation times if possible. Teachers agreed to send assignments with families if children had to miss school days.
- Parents didn't understand how their children were learning to read; it was different from instruction in Mexico. Teachers explained and invited parents in to observe practices such as word walls, read-alouds, and classroom libraries. The local League of United Latin American Citizens provided translators.
- The school library became more central to learning when they purchased books in Spanish for families to read to children, and encouraged parents to check out books in English for their children to read to them. (Henderson et al., 2007)

In this chapter we'll examine what your school counts as parental involvement and what steps you might take to refocus those efforts on student learning. When you do, you just might find what families and teachers at McCoy Elementary found—reading achievement goes up (Henderson et al., 2007).

DISCUSS PARENTAL INVOLVEMENT PRACTICES AT YOUR SCHOOL

Packaged programs, whether they are focused on involving parents or improving reading, often insult the intelligence of teachers and ignore the history of hard work in schools. You haven't picked this book up saying, "Gee, involving families in their children's learning—I never thought about that."

My guess is that your school is like many of the schools I work with. You have created multiple ways of involving parents, from breakfasts to conferences to programs featuring their children. You may write newsletters, send home agendas, or call parents with good news. In fact, if your school is like many schools, you may feel overwhelmed with all that your school is doing and underwhelmed with the response from families.

Let's look at what you are doing. Start with brainstorming. Work in small groups. Write down everything that your school and you as an individual are doing to involve families. These can be schoolwide, like Family Night, or specific to one classroom. They can be formal events or informal practices, like chatting with parents when they pick their kids up from school. I've facilitated this inventory process with whole school faculties, individual teachers, grade-level groups, and groups of teachers and parents together—I highly recommend the latter. (See online supplementary materials for parents at http://www.tcpress.com.)

You are going to be amazed when you see these lists. I haven't worked with a group yet where the list didn't cover at least one sheet of paper. Most schools are working really hard to connect with families. But don't stop there. Ask each group to put the items on the brainstorming list in one of three columns: (1) Supports Student Learning; (2) Builds Deeper Relationships; (3) Does Neither (but we keep doing it anyway).

Next, create a 3-column chart from all of the separate charts. Some practices may be in both Columns 1 and 2—bravo if you are doing things that both build relationships and increase learning! Some practices may end up in all three columns, because you may have very different perspectives across groups—a teacher may believe that parent conferences both support increased learning and build deeper relationships, but a father states strongly that in his opinion it does neither. A principal may view Open House as supporting student achievement by telling parents about curriculum; teachers might argue that the current format does allow for meaningful conversations about learning. Teachers at different grade levels might similarly disagree. These debates open the door to discuss new practices: Under what circumstances, for which families and students, with what kind of structure can parent conferences, for example, lead to increased literacy learning? If you send home newsletters, are they one-way communications, or do they invite families to respond? Are they focused on what students are learning or on "school business" information?

Table 1.1 is a partial list that one group of elementary teachers generated. They taught in high-poverty schools in urban and rural settings. They worked with very different communities and school environments. Notice how many practices appear across all three columns.

TABLE 1.1. Example of Analysis of Current Family Involvement Efforts

Leads to Increased Learning	Leads to Deeper Relationships	Does Neither (but we keep doing it anyway)
Parent conferences	Parent conferences	Parent conferences
Parent folders, agendas	Parent folders, agendas	Parent folders, agendas
Communication such as phone calls, newsletters, e-mails, good news cards	Communication such as phone calls, newsletters, e-mails, good news cards	Communication such as phone calls, newsletters, e-mails, good news cards
Family Literacy Night	Home visits	Family Literacy Night
Home visits	Family journals	School programs, talent shows, festivals, Field Day, International Day
Family journals	Grandparents Day, Dads Day, Heritage Day (e.g., Latino, Black, rural)	Open House, Information Night, Ice Cream Social, Donuts for Dad/Muffins for Mom/Granola for Grandparents
Writing marathon, students and parents writing together at school		

EXPLORE PARTNERSHIPS
THAT LEAD TO LITERACY LEARNING

Now that you have a sense of where you are as a school, where do you want to go?

Anne Henderson and Karen Mapp (2002) synthesized 80 studies on parental involvement, preschool through high school, in settings throughout the United States. In the excellent book that grew out of this research, *Beyond the Bake Sale* (Henderson et al., 2007), they concluded: "The evidence is consistent, positive, and convincing: families have a major influence on their children's achievement. When schools, families, and community groups work together to support learning, children tend to do better in school, stay in school longer, and like school more" (p. 2).

The critical factor that increased student learning was when parental involvement was directly related to their children's academic learning. It sounds so obvious, but think back to your three-column chart: How many activities are in that third column, events that take a great deal of time and energy from teachers or parents or both, but have nothing to do with learning?

Before we go back to that chart, let's look at Henderson and Mapp's (2002) key findings:

- Programs and interventions that engage families in supporting their children's learning at home are linked to improved student achievement.
- The more families support their children's learning and educational progress, both in quantity and over time, the more their children tend to do well in school and continue their education.
- Families of all cultural backgrounds, education, and income levels can, and often do, have a positive influence on their children's learning.
- Family and community involvement that is linked to student learning has a greater effect on achievement than more general forms of involvement.

Someone might look at those findings and think, "Homework! That's the answer. I send lots of it home, and expect all parents in my culturally and economically diverse classroom to help their children with it. I seem to have the perfect parent involvement program—except that only about half my students do their homework." Read on.

We need to examine another critical conclusion Henderson and Mapp (2002) reached: "When programs and initiatives focus on building respectful and trusting relationships among school staff, families, and community members, they are more effective in creating and sustaining connections that support student achievement" (p. 43). Across studies the authors learned some critical points:

- Programs that successfully connect with families and community invite involvement, are welcoming, and address specific parental and community needs.
- Parent involvement programs that are effective in engaging diverse families recognize cultural and class differences, address needs, and build on strengths.
- Effective connections embrace a philosophy of partnership where power is shared—the responsibility for children's

educational development is a collaborative enterprise
among parents, school staff, and community members.

It's not as easy as sending home reading logs to sign or spelling lists to study. Learning will not necessarily increase with the
number of parents who come to PTA meetings, Donuts for Dad
breakfasts, or even parent–teacher conferences. We have to build
relationships, build on cultural and social class strengths, respond
to specific family needs, and share the power of creating learning
opportunities.

Kathleen Hoover-Dempsey, Joan Walker, and Howard Sandler
(2005) are psychologists who studied what motivates parents to
take active roles in their children's learning. A key factor is a feeling
of self-efficacy: "I know my action made a difference for my child's
learning." Parental self-efficacy can develop from different experiences. Undoubtedly, the most powerful is experiencing success in
helping their child learn, and expressing it: "You have such interesting insights about the characters in this story, Nisha. I'm so glad
we read and talked about it together." The authors suggest that parents also build self-efficacy by observing other parents—especially
parents in their own school—successfully helping students, and by
receiving encouragement from people who are important to them
(e.g., their child's teacher, another parent). The authors provide
four touchstones for developing respectful family–school partnerships focused on learning. Under each touchstone I quote specific
advice from Hoover-Dempsey et al. (2005, p. 49), followed by my
literacy examples in italics, many of which we'll explore in detail in
subsequent chapters (noted in parentheses).

1. Enact the values, expectations, and behaviors that enable
   parent-school partnership.
   a. "Believe and communicate that parents have an
      important role to play in their children's educational
      success." *Share with parents that the reading, writing,
      viewing, listening, and talking they do in their everyday
      lives (e.g., reading advertising fliers or church liturgies), and
      in whatever language they speak at home, will support their
      children's literacy development (Chapter 3).*
   b. "Offer specific information about ways in which
      parents' active engagement in children's schooling
      supports student learning." *Offer opportunities like*

family–school reading journals (Chapter 5) or family-
teacher-student writing projects (Chapter 6).

c. "Create and maintain a school environment that
    overtly values and respects parental presence and
    input." *Seek parental ideas and participation in creating
    culturally rich classroom and hall displays of learning. Make
    the library available and useful to families. Provide space
    and time for informal chats about student literacy learning
    (Chapter 2).*

2. Offer opportunities to help children learn successfully,
    to observe other parents or adults who are successfully
    helping students learning, . . . [and] to receive
    encouragement when doubts or obstacles arise.

    a. "Communicate with parents about the positive
        influence of varied parental involvement behaviors on
        student attributes that lead to student school success."
        *You might say, "Going over the reading assignment each
        night is really helping Sabrina take more care with her
        homework," or "Roberto is writing much longer, more
        detailed stories these days—I think it really impressed him
        when you talked about how persistent you have to be in your
        job as a food inspector."*

    b. "Use existing parent–teacher structures to enhance
        involvement." *Reconceptualize parent–teacher conferences,
        Open House, and other school events to focus on
        partnerships for literacy learning (Chapters 2 and 8).*

    c. "Give parents specific feedback on the positive
        influence of their involvement activities." *When family
        members share their knowledge in a curriculum unit, write
        about photographs, or participate in family–school reading
        journals, follow up with specific feedback about what
        difference it made for their child (Chapters 4–6).*

3. Convey that parental involvement is expected and wanted,
    that involvement is important to the children's success,
    and that parents' activities at home and at school are
    all important contributors to their child's learning and
    success:

    a. "Develop overtly welcoming practices that respect
        and build on family culture and strengths." *Invite
        parents to "Tell me about your child." Make family visits,
        learn family stories, and incorporate family funds of
        knowledge (Chapters 2–3).*

    b. "Seek, develop, and welcome involvement

that engages parents and teachers in two-way communications." *Develop newsletters, weekly reports, or quarterly assessments that invite parents to write or tape-record responses. For example, after a newsletter section on an author study of Donald Crews, invite family members to comment on trips to visit a relative* (Bigmama's, 1998) *or lessons learned from family elders* (Shortcut, 1996). *Invite parents to help develop goals and actions for their child's literacy learning (Chapter 8).*

   c. "Offer a full range of home-based and school-based involvement opportunities; advertise them clearly, attractively, and repeatedly." *I hope you find many ideas you can make your own throughout this book!*

4. Help students convey that parental involvement is expected, wanted, and valuable.

   a. "Develop interactive homework assignments." *Plan meaningful "home" work with students, which asks them to involve their parents or other family or adult mentors. A good resource is the Teachers Involve Parents in Schoolwork (TIPS) Web site featuring homework that requires students to talk with someone at home about what they are learning at school (www.csos.jhu.edu/P2000/tips/languagearts.htm). When students have this responsibility, it is more likely to be effective than a note from you stuffed in a backpack.*

   b. "Encourage student-parent conversations about school activities." *Help students take the initiative. As the day ends, have students write down for their families the two most interesting or important things they did or learned that day on a sticky note or piece of recycled scrap paper. Or use "weekend journals" to invite conversations about the major learning focus for the week (Chapter 5).*

This is a lot of advice to incorporate all at once. Where's a place to start? In your study groups you might write these four touchstones, listing the strategies under each on large charts. Give everyone three dots and ask them to "vote" with the dots. Voters may place the dots on three different strategies they want to explore, or all three on one strategy if they feel really strongly about it. It might be helpful to give each grade level a different color of dots to see if there are different priorities for different grade levels. For example, if most of the yellow (kindergarten) and blue (third grade) dots are clustered around family visits, those teachers might begin there. Or there may be interest across the school in one area, perhaps student-led conferences. You'll be able to see at a glance where people are most invested and form study teams based on genuine interest.

ACT TO EXPLORE LITERACY LEARNING PARTNERSHIPS

As you talk about these powerful findings, go back to your three-column chart. What questions do you have? How might you address the frustrations of Column 3, events which you have spent hours each year organizing, inviting, and staffing, but which some group members believe do not really lead to either stronger relationships or increased learning?

You might be interested in some of the questions the elementary teachers who generated Table 1.1 asked:

- *Parent conferences.* Could we shift from only reporting past learning to supporting new learning? Could parents play a more active role? Could students?
- *Communication such as phone calls, newsletters, e-mails, good news cards.* Could we shift focus to literacy learning? How can we involve families through newsletters, rather than just telling them what we've done or plan to do?
- *School programs, talent shows, festivals, Field Day, International Day.* Could parents and teachers together make these learning, not just performing, events? Why don't we focus on the countries from which our students have immigrated for International Day? Could parents be talent show coaches for singing, dancing, art? How can we draw on parents' sports expertise during Field Day?
- *Open House, Information Night, Ice Cream Social.* How could we learn about parents' strengths and interests? Could we schedule small groups rather than "drop in any time" to get to know parents? Could parents participate in a short literature circle or writing workshop with their kids?
- *Donuts for Dad/Muffins for Mom/Granola for Grandparents.* Could we have a literacy focus, for example, phonemic-awareness games, creating child or family books, kids interviewing family members about various topics? Could we invite families to our classrooms rather than the

cafeteria so teachers, parents, and students can get to know each other?

There is another alternative for activities in Column 3—drop them! Just because you've always done it doesn't mean you have to continue. Schools are infamous for adding on new programs and practices without discarding old ones. Here's an opportunity to reclaim time for new, more effective strategies in Columns 1 and 2.

You are at the beginning of an exciting process, one where teachers and parents can really make a difference for children as they become confident and engaged readers and writers.

READ TO LEARN MORE

Henderson, A., Mapp, K., Johnson, V., & Davies, D. (2007). *Beyond the bake sale: The essential guide to family–school partnerships.* New York: The New Press.

> Building on their research findings, the authors include sections on building relationships, linking parent involvement to learning, sharing power, and addressing racial, class, and cultural differences. They include research, examples of successful practices, and tools such as checklists and surveys.

Delgado Gaitan, C. (2004). *Involving Latino families in schools: Raising student achievement through home-school partnerships.* Thousand Oaks, CA: Corwin Press.

> With rich examples from her many years of working with Latino communities, Delgado Gaitan takes a strengths-based approach that builds on family language, culture, history, and values. She includes many specific examples of communication practices and educational programs.

Allen, J. (2007). *Creating welcoming schools: A practical guide to home-school partnerships with diverse families.* New York: Teachers College Press.

> A little self promotion here, but teachers and families have found this to be a useful, in-depth look at partnerships. In addition to some of the practices in this current volume, *Creating Welcoming Schools* discusses exploring memories of schooling, writing cultural memoirs, and the critical role of dialogue in establishing trusting relationships.

Develop Trusting Relationships

I have always spent time at the beginning of the year getting to know the children: talking to them, listening to them as they play, as they talk to their friends, as they try to tell me who they are. But this year . . . I asked the parents to tell me who their children were: what they loved, what they hated, what they were afraid of, what made them angry . . . and what the parents wanted for them, what their goals were, their hopes, their concerns. Some wrote long letters, others called me on the phone, others came and talked before and after school. So I'm getting to know them—and love them—a lot more quickly than other years. (Mary Ginley, quoted in Nieto, 1999, p. 100)

W HO KNOWS A child better than family? Whether students have been living with parents, grandparents, foster parents, or in some other family arrangement, they have lives outside of school that we need to understand in order to teach them most effectively. Yet most beginning-of-school rituals—Open House, Back to School Night, Meet Your Teacher Day—focus on what the child and family need to know, bring, and do "so we can have a successful school year."

As the mother of three children, I attended many such events. I have been greeted with hugs by teachers I knew, had regulations and procedures explained to me ad nauseam, been entertained by witty teachers talking about special events, been urged (unsuccessfully) to sign discipline agreements, and been inundated with lists of supplies, rules, and layers of consequences for breaking said rules. I have never been asked, "Tell me about your child."

DISCUSS HOW WE CAN LEARN ABOUT EACH OTHER

In this chapter let's think together about how you want to start the year. Here are some questions that you might discuss in grade levels, at a faculty meeting, and preferably in a group with parents as well as teachers. (See online supplementary materials for parents at http://www.tcpress.com.) The face teachers and principals think they show to the community may be very different from the face individual families see when they come to your school.

1. Is our building a welcoming place for all families? Is it accessible to people in wheelchairs, people with strollers? Are all signs and labels in the languages families speak? Do the walls represent the cultures of all families in terms of artwork, books and other materials on display, and community events posted? Are posted messages positive and inviting (e.g., "Our library is a family library— come check out a book or video!") or regulatory and disciplinary (e.g., "Only two books per week. Penalty for overdue books!")

2. Who are the people (principal, teachers, aides, older students, other parents) who greet families at Open House, on the first day of school, on every day of school? What do we see as our role (directing traffic, moving people

efficiently, or making people feel genuinely welcome)? Do we (collectively) speak the languages of families? Do we stop to listen if a parent needs to talk? Do we make an effort to learn names not only of children but also of other family members? Do we smile? At everyone?

3. What is the purpose of the first family event (e.g., Open House)? Is it one-way communication, mostly "telling"? How might we restructure this event to generate two-way communication? How might we learn about our new students from their families? How might we start building relationships with the families who will make up our extended learning community for the next 9 months?

EXPLORE WAYS TEACHERS AND FAMILIES BUILD COMMUNITY

How do we first communicate with families? Is it a letter, flyer, or newspaper or radio announcement about the beginning of school or Open House? Are we reaching all families? Is it invitational? Teachers all over the country create ways to connect with students and families early each school year. In this section we'll examine several that you might modify and make your own.

Issue Multiple Invitations

Not every family will respond to every invitation, so it's important to issue several. Teacher-researcher Stephanie Jones (2006) taught Grades 1–5 in a working-poor neighborhood where families sometimes disliked or feared teachers. She worked hard to establish relationships with multiple invitations: a welcoming open-door policy, home-school weekly journals, flexible parent–teacher conferences, and home visits. Most important in breaking down barriers were her weekly positive phone calls and notes. "I was no longer perceived as the enemy . . . I located positive attributes in their child and genuinely *liked* him or her" (p. 110).

In addition to these invitations, you might consider the following as well.

Letter to the Child Before School Starts. Molly Rose, who taught in both suburban and urban schools, created multiple opportunities to dialogue with parents throughout the year (Lawrence-Lightfoot, 2003). Molly wrote to each child before school started telling what she did during the summer, e.g., "I read a lot of good books, I went swimming, and I went hiking" (p. 62). She drew a picture of herself hiking, and asked the children to draw pictures of themselves and have an adult help them write to her. When families came to school, these letters decorated the classroom.

Getting-to-Know-You Conferences. Molly also invited each parent or guardian to come in sometime during the first month. "This is purely a listening conference . . . . The parents are the experts, and I'm seeking their wisdom and their guidance . . . . I'm saying come and tell me all about your child," Molly said (Lawrence-Lightfoot, 2003, p. 62). She got 100% participation because, as she explained, "I make myself available any time of the day. . . . When they break an appointment or do not show, . . . I don't take it personally. We work until we can find another time" (p. 63).

"Tell Me About Your Child." Like Mary Ginley at the beginning of this chapter and many other teachers around the country, Betty Shockley (1st grade) and Barbara Michalove (2nd grade) began the year with a written invitation to parents to "Please tell me about your child" (Shockley, Michalove, & Allen, 1995).

Every family wrote back. Parents in this working-class, predominantly African American neighborhood poured out their hopes, insights, advice, and anxieties. A theme—Our child is special and very dear to us—echoed across the letters. Janice Barnett's pride in her daughter was evident:

> Lakendra Echols is very witty. She likes to go to movies, and she like to go to the mall especially the toy store. And most of all she likes to help with the house work. Washing dishes the most. Lakendra like to be my big girl; she's very out-spoken about what's she feel. Me and Lakendra have no secrets from each other. I can trust my big girl and she can count on me. She's my little star. (Schockley et al., 1995, p. 41)

This simple invitation can be issued in person at a family visit before school starts, in a letter (translated in each parent's home language, with an invitation to respond in that language), or by e-mail or a class blog if *all* parents have access.

Rethink Open House,
Meet Your Teacher, or Back to School Night

In every group of teachers I've worked with who have done the three-column analysis of their school's parental involvement initiatives (see Chapter 1), at least some of them have put Open House in the third column. This beginning of school ritual often fails to realize its potential. How can we restructure such events to be a foundation for building relationships with families and focus on student learning?

Sudia Paloma McCaleb (1997) shared the letter one teacher (who is not named) wrote to families before Back to School Night:

> Dear Parents of Room 4,
>
> It has been a pleasure to begin to get to know your children during this first week of school. They are so bright-eyed and seem so ready to learn. I know we are going to have an exciting year together.
>
> As your child's first teacher, I know that you have taught her a great deal. I hope that we can talk soon and that you can share with me some of the ways in which you have taught your child at home. I'm sure that you will have good suggestions about what you want your child to learn at school and how I, as her new teacher, can help her to learn better.
>
> We have a bulletin board in our classroom which we have saved for pictures of our students and their families. We would love for each student to bring to the classroom a picture of the special adults in her life. In that way the students will feel your presence and know that your support is there while they are learning at school. (p. 34)

Look at all this teacher accomplished in terms of inviting a partnership with families: She let parents know that she valued the children, acknowledged parents as important teachers of their children, invited them to share suggestions on how to teach their child, and invited them to have a presence in the classroom both physically and with their pictures. Note that she did not ask for "each student to bring a picture of his mom and dad"; she recognized families have different structures.

At Back to School Night a few weeks later, families gathered at the bulletin board and began making connections, talking about

the pictures and their children. The pictures served not only to connect teachers, students, and families, but also to connect families
with each other. The teacher then gathered everyone to discuss how
they would work together during the year. She recognized them
as their children's first teachers and acknowledged that they may
have wounds from their own schooling. Then the teacher explained
the family book authoring project She shared a book she had written about herself, her cultural influences, and her own family, and
she asked for their feedback. The book contained photographs and
short text written in both English and Spanish, since the teacher
was bilingual. She explained that they would have several opportunities during the year to create similar books with their children,
and with her support. I discuss a similar process by Ada and Campoy (2004) in Chapter 6.

Finally, the teacher asked the parents what they felt would be
important for their children to learn that school year. Although tim-
id at first—after all, they were not used to a teacher asking them
what to teach!—parents eventually generated a list that included
"reading, writing, respect, English, and getting along with other
children" (McCaleb, 1997, p. 35). One interesting development that
grew out of this multilayered Back to School night was that two
Spanish-speaking mothers began coming to the classroom every
day to help the teacher and to learn English along with their children.

Want to take a smaller step? Henderson et al. (2007) report that
principal Karl Smith holds an Open House for each grade level on
different nights. That way teachers who are often left out—such
as art, music, special education, and media specialists—can meet
more families, teachers and families have time for in-depth sharing
like McCaleb described, and families with several children don't
have to run from room to room.

Make School Gatherings Culturally Inclusive

One of the main goals of beginning-of-school gatherings is to
make each family feel welcome and valued. How do we think, talk,
and plan specifically for inclusivity? Ellen Kahn, Director of the Human Rights Campaign Family Project, noted that research "shows
links between academic achievement, emotional well-being and
an inclusive school climate" (Human Rights Campaign Founda-

tion, p. 7). Only about 25% of children are being raised in "house-holds headed by a married, heterosexual couple"; consequently "it is deeply important that all children attend schools in which they learn to appreciate and respect human differences, and see their own families reflected in the tapestry of the diverse school community" (p. 7).

We need to look at our schools through the eyes of our students' families. Children may live in foster, one-parent, grandparent, two-mom or two-dad, stepparent, or multigenerational families. Family structures may be temporarily or permanently affected by prison, war, homelessness, or physical or mental illness. Are they represented in the books in classroom libraries, read-aloud selection, and projects like the ubiquitous beginning-of-year kindergarten unit on families? Do we need to revise forms, such as those that ask for names of Mother and Father rather than the more open-ended Parent/Guardian? How can our schools be truly welcoming of all families?

Family Diversity Tree. One California elementary school family dinner focused on their Family Diversity Tree. Each child contributed a leaf with his or her family composition. The principal selected several families to speak. A multiracial family explained how they wanted their children to be connected to the cultures and religions of both parents. A daughter of a family parented by two mothers said, "We are no different than other families." Another young woman in a wheelchair shared how her mother took good care of her. Other children spoke too, with the common themes of "my parents care for me" and "we have lots of fun together" (Human Rights Campaign Foundation, 2009, p. 11).

Neighborhood Maps. Another way for families and educators to get to know each other early in the year is through drawing neighborhood maps (Frank, 2003). Neighborhood maps are a wonderful activity for beginning-of-school gatherings for a variety of reasons: Some people are more comfortable drawing than writing; it's fun as well as informative; adults and kids become equals; and families and teachers learn about each other through storytelling. What would your map include? Did you move from another state or country? How were you and your family treated? How were you known as a kid? Are there messages inscribed on the sidewalks, the apartment walls, or your memory about being a girl or boy, Jewish or Methodist, English- or Spanish- or Japanese-speaking?

Sharing the maps in small groups of teachers, parents, and children could lead to a class book, with students interviewing their parents about their childhood neighborhoods, or writing "Then and Now" comparisons. One of the most enjoyable ways I've drawn these maps with groups of teachers and parents is with sidewalk chalk. After 15 minutes of drawing maps on the sidewalk, everyone walks around looking at each other's maps, asking questions, making connections. Imagine if a whole school did this on the sidewalks, asphalt, or even the outside walls of the school (hey, it's bound to rain sometime) on Back to School Night! (See online supplementary materials for parents.)

Sharing Stories of Schooling. The beginning-of-school event may end with the neighborhood maps and sharing, but I'd encourage you to consider a next step in building relationships. When families return to the classroom, guide (and contribute to) discussion of these three questions:

1. What is a happy memory you have of school when you were your child's age?
2. What is an unhappy memory you have of school?
3. What would you like your child's memory of this year to be? What are your hopes for his or her experience in this class?

If there is time, suggest that parents talk to each other in pairs or small groups, then ask for volunteers as the whole group comes together. Some parents may not want to share negative experiences with anyone; one teacher recently told me with visible pain and anger that she would not revisit her racist elementary years. Sharing can be awkward if the negative experiences were at your school, with a colleague; ask people please not to use names of teachers in the school. These risks are real. However, they are outweighed by the benefits in building trusting, supportive relationships among the important adults in each child's life.

Visiting Family Neighborhoods. No, this is not the drive-by bus tour. This is the walking tour, with students and family members, and perhaps staff who live in the neighborhood as guides. While you may need a bus to take you to one or more neighborhoods, it's the on-the-ground interaction that's important.

Bruce-Monroe Elementary School in Washington, D.C., includes African American, Central American, and Vietnamese families. If it is like the majority of urban schools, few of its teachers live in the neighborhood. Before school starts, "families, teachers, children, administrators, custodians, kitchen workers, and front office staff" gather at the school for a "Community Walk" led by parents and a custodian from the neighborhood (Henderson et al., 2007, p. 137). They visit community food markets, repair shops, an African bookstore, houses, apartment buildings, and the tiny parks where children play. They return to the school for lunch and chatting about "their" neighborhood. Teachers learned about community resources, met community members, and started the school year with new relationships already established.

Collaborating with Interpreters. At school gatherings and particularly individual conferences, schools where teachers and families don't speak the same language need to provide interpreters. Bilingual interpreters may come from the school or the district, or they may be high school or college students, or community members. Fay and Whaley (2004), elementary ESOL teachers, offer excellent advice for working with an interpreter:

1. Ask about how many sentences to say before pausing for translation.
2. Ask how to say a few common phrases of greeting, encouragement, and so on.
3. Look at the parent or family member, not the interpreter, throughout the conference.

If no one can interpret at a school gathering, make family members welcome, smile, point to student work, smile some more, show them the room. It's a start.

ACT TO BUILD RELATIONSHIPS

There are so many possibilities and no one right place to start— only the right place for *you* to start. We haven't even talked about what may be the most effective way of building strong, respectful relationships: family (home) visits. They deserve their own chapter—and it's the next one.

In thinking about next steps, start with what you are already doing and what you might stop, add, or revise with the goal of building strong relationships.

Individual teachers might:

- Invite parents or other family members to "tell me about your child" in person or in a short letter
- Schedule "getting-to-know-you-conferences" during preplanning—maybe parents can help you organize the room!
- Revise the scheduled time for families such as Open House to draw neighborhood maps, tell stories of schooling, or introduce projects in which families will be involved, like coauthoring books.

Whole school faculties or parent–teacher councils might:

- Study the purpose, structure, and effectiveness of current Open House or similar events; discuss, gather input, and reenvision
- Plan a Community Walk
- Plan a Family Diversity event

READ TO LEARN MORE

Fay, K., & Whaley, S. (2004). *Becoming one community: Reading and writing with English language learners.* Portland, ME: Stenhouse.

The authors are experienced elementary ESOL teachers. Their Chapter 12, "Making Home-School Connections," includes suggestions for back-to-school night, innovative open houses, and excellent ideas for extending into the community, such as offering homework help in a community center and after-school clubs that promote native-language literacy.

CHAPTER 3

Build on Family Knowledge, Languages, and Literacies

At dinner [my father] spoke very little. One night his children and even his wife helplessly giggled at his garbled English pronunciation of the Catholic Grace before Meals. Thereafter he made his wife recite the prayer at the start of each meal. (Rodriguez, 1982, p. 24)

HOME LANGUAGE. It's a comforting phrase, isn't it, conjuring images of families chatting around the television, dinner table, or front porch; of dads or grandmas telling stories about relatives' escapades, of moms or grandpas crooning the baby to sleep; of siblings and cousins making up games and arguing about the rules. Yet too often in our country's educational history, we have at best ignored home language as a valuable linguistic resource and at worst denigrated and even prohibited its use in school. Some schools expect teachers to "correct" student dialects when they vary from "book English" (Delpit, 1995), and to emphasize "English only" as soon as possible for newcomers. Some teachers have even asked parents to speak English at home to help their child assimilate, as Richard Rodriguez's teachers told his father.

Home literacies. Do we envision them for our students' families? Denny Taylor and Catherine Dorsey-Gaines (1988) spent many hours with African American families living in an urban neighborhood and documented an extensive array of literacies: reading magazines, books, newspapers, applications, church newsletters, textbooks for college courses, and neighborhood fliers for meetings or missing children; writing lists, budgets, applications, poetry, college papers, and letters to teachers, prisoners, friends, and their children. Today we'd add the explosion of digital literacies—text messages, blogs, games, Internet sites, videos, e-mail.

I worry that we sometimes get so caught up in school language and literacies that we may not take the time to learn those of families. Yet this is the essential starting point for educating all children—what they bring with them to school. In this chapter we'll explore ways of learning family languages and literacies, and how we build on this wealth of knowledge students bring to our classrooms.

DISCUSS HOW YOU CURRENTLY
BUILD ON FAMILY LANGUAGES AND LITERACIES

Some questions for discussion:

1. How do we learn about what families know, their home language(s), and their home literacies? Make a list.
2. How complete and accurate are our current sources? Analyze the list with some honest school soul-searching: How helpful and accurate are impressions of families

we get from school records, comments from colleagues, conversations with family members?

3. How much do we learn about family languages and literacies from current sources? What more do we need to learn?

EXPLORE FAMILY FUNDS OF KNOWLEDGE

The list, analysis, and discussion in the previous section probably led to a fourth question: What are other teachers doing to learn about family language, literacy, and learning? Let's explore.

Learning Family Funds of Knowledge

The concept of family "funds of knowledge" was developed by researchers in a project that began in Tucson, Arizona, with a group of teachers and anthropology and education professors who challenged the deficit model of families and children. Their goal of learning from families was "to alter perceptions of working-class or poor communities and to view these households primarily in terms of their strengths and resources (or funds of knowledge)" (Gonzáles, Moll, & Amanti, 2005, p. x).

Teachers in the original funds of knowledge study group served working-class Mexican and Yaqui Indian families. They created meaningful relationships with families by visiting homes, usually of three children each year. Teachers first studied both the history of that border-region community and the labor histories of the families (especially mining and agriculture). During the home visits they talked with (rather than interviewed) families. The conversations centered around three main areas of information, usually gathered in three visits: (1) family history and work history; (2) routine household activities; and (3) parents' views on raising children, languages used at home, and schooling.

Families had a wealth of knowledge about ranching, farming, mining, construction, and repair. Their business knowledge included appraising, renting and selling, labor laws, and building codes. Household management acumen included budgeting, child care, cooking, and repair. Many had knowledge of both contemporary and folk medicine—for people as well as animals. Religious knowledge included rituals, texts (especially the Bible), and moral and ethical understandings. The authors stressed that the primary purpose of their home visits was "to foster a relationship of trust with the families" (Gonzáles et al., 2005, p. xi).

Teachers met throughout the year to discuss what they learned and to create thematic units of study based on family funds of knowledge, as we'll see in the next section. It is helpful to consider four key findings from the work of Gonzáles et al. (2005) as we think about forming relationships with families that support children's learning:

1. *All* families have important experiences, skills, and bodies of knowledge.
2. Families use these funds of knowledge through social networks of family and friends, often including multiple people outside the home.
3. Teachers learn about *how* children learn.
4. *Confianza*—mutual trust—is essential in establishing relationships. Creating "reciprocity" (a healthy interdependency) is critical for enduring relationships; both teachers and parents "give" in ways that support each other, and that support the child's learning.

Classroom Funds of Knowledge Projects

Cathy Amanti (2005), a multiage, intermediate-grades bilingual teacher in Tucson, detailed one curriculum unit she and her students developed. That year, Cathy visited three homes and found a surprising commonality: horses. The Alfaros family owned three horses just a few blocks from the school; "Mr. Alfaro is teaching all his sons how to care for and ride horses. He himself is teaching his horse to dance. . . . Mr. Alfaro participated in rodeos in Mexico" (p. 133). Fernando rode and cared for horses each summer when he returned to stay with his grandparents on their ranch in Chihuahua. At the Rivera home, the family was watching a video a relative had taped of a horse race in Sonoyta, Mexico.

Based on this information, Cathy asked her class to write about their knowledge of horses. She learned that many of her students were interested in horses and knew a great deal about them. Together, they planned an integrated unit on horses. They built on their own extensive background knowledge, generated sophisticated questions, and conducted inquiry projects that integrated three subject areas:

- Social studies (e.g., Spanish explorers and missionaries, history of saddles, local horse ordinances)
- Language arts (e.g., online and library research, English/ Spanish vocabulary, written and oral presentations)
- Science and math (e.g., horse anatomy, multicelled organisms, converting "hands" to inches and feet, and horse gestation and evolution)

Families served as resources to their children both on individual projects and in whole-class learning, which included a live horse-shoeing demonstration, a field trip to see the Alfarso horses, and the home video of the Mexican horse race. Students learned, parents were valuable partners, and relationships deepened, all from incorporating family funds of knowledge.

In a multicultural Tucson classroom kindergarten teacher Marla Hensley (2005) found a wealth of talent on home visits with Alicia, one of her African American students. Marla learned that Alicia's father, Jacob, a groundskeeper who had helped the class plant a garden, played guitar and keyboard and wrote poetry and songs. At Marla's invitation, Jacob and the kindergartners wrote a musical version of "The Little Red Hen" that combined gardening, music, and the study of bread making in various cultures. A home visit with another family revealed an African American foster parent skilled in dance; she choreographed the musical. Marla enlisted family members as costume makers, stagehands, makeup experts, and bread makers of different kinds of bread including Navajo fry bread and tortillas. Jacob eventually became PTA president and one of the school's most eloquent advocates.

Teachers in other parts of the country are also learning about specific family funds of knowledge in their neighborhoods.

- Teachers in New York City visiting Puerto Rican households learned of extensive family funds of knowledge. These included information about countries in Latin America, electrical wiring, music and dance (classical, jazz, salsa), computer technology, sales (e.g., Avon, Tupperware), needlework, teaching, translation and interpretation, diet and health, and community advocacy work (Mercado, 2005).
- Teachers I talked with in Tooksook Bay, Alaska, identified knowledge among the Yup'ik Eskimo residents including

small engine repair, exquisite tundra grass basket weaving, and fishing skills such as making and repairing hooks and nets, as well as catching, curing, and cooking fish. Further, young Yup'iks learn primarily from observation and trial and error; verbal instruction is less important. This tradition led Tooksook Bay teachers to provide more opportunities for students to observe and approximate certain academic skills, rather than relying on verbal explanations of concepts.

• Teachers in an Appalachian region of Kentucky learned who, when, if, and how parents helped their children with homework. They learned that social, emotional, and academic needs might not be evident at school. Families shared knowledge such as farming procedures and the inner workings of the Veterans Administration. This information influenced a myriad of teaching decisions, from what kind of work went home with certain children, to a unit on "Animals at Home," to Agricultural Field Day involving community members (McIntyre, Kyle, Moore, Sweazy, & Greer, 2001).

Building on Family Languages and Literacies

In an illuminating review of research, Sonia Nieto (1999) concluded that proficiency in and use of the home language correlated positively with learning in school; this was true in studies of native Spanish speakers, speakers of African American Vernacular English (AAVE), and others. There is evidence that families often suffer "serious disruptions" when children "learned English in school and lost their native language." Nieto's strong recommendation: Encourage families "to speak their native language with their children, to speak it often, and to use it consistently" (p. 93).

Similarly, in his summary of research on learning vocabulary Michael Graves (2006) concluded: "Students need to develop their oral language skills in both their native language and in English. Research clearly shows that strong language skills in the native language facilitate students' reading in English" (p. 34). If only Richard Rodriguez's teachers had known this research! As Nieto (1999) poignantly observed, "Doing away with a language, or prohibiting its use, tears away at the soul of a people" (p. 60)

There is another consideration crucial to student learning: When children and family members can talk freely, without worrying about whether they are speaking "proper" English, they are much more likely to have conversations that support learning. Sometimes that support is direct, as when the child shares the spellbinding book she is reading or translates her classroom newspaper article into Korean for her grandmother. Just as important are the everyday conversations and rituals where language is central.

Teachers have not only the opportunity but the obligation to help parents recognize the power of their home-language interactions with their children. Even when teachers are highly supportive of students' home language, family members, especially those new to the United States, may get the message from neighbors, previous immigrants, and the media that maintaining their home language is an impediment to their child's success. There are similar negative messages about Black, Appalachian, and other dialects. Teachers have a difficult but critical challenge: to help students learn "edited English" in speaking and writing, but also maintain their home language, and develop the social and linguistic skills to know when to use which. Whew—that's a tall order for teachers and students!

What are some ways parents, teachers, and students can study these politically charged and personally vital language issues? Drawing on excellent suggestions from Clara Alexander (1980) for language study with speakers of Black English, or AAVE dialects, I selected the following from her article and adapted them to include family involvement. You can modify this language study for different ages, and to include the home languages and dialects of your students.

1. Read or listen to speeches, stories, and poems written by African American politicians, authors, and poets. Family members or community figures such as preachers could serve as oratory coaches as students learn to perform self-selected poems or speeches.
2. Send a variety of linguistically diverse literature home; ask families to read aloud together and discuss how authors use languages and dialect for literary purposes.
3. First as a class, then in small groups, then at home with family members, ask students to translate short passages from stories written in AAVE into "edited English," and

different passages written in "edited English" into AAVE. Discuss authors' decisions about language use, and relate to students' own writing for various purposes and audiences.

4. Have students conduct a TV survey with a parent or other family member, noting which programs use various languages and dialects, why, and what message the audience gets about the characters from their language.
5. Role-play and discuss situations in which AAVE and edited English would be used. Interview parents about when and how they "switch codes."
6. Ask students to read drafts of their writing aloud with an adult and discuss language choices.

Jacqueline Jordan Irvine's (1990) award-winning review of policies and practices that led to increased learning for Black students also pinpoints strategies for building on family language and literacies. She recommended that teachers include chanting, storytelling, choral responses, and incorporating the music children listen to at home. Many of these elements are embodied in hip-hop culture. While we older folks (speaking as a grandma) may associate it with youth culture, many elementary students' parents are part of the hip-hop generation. Hip-hop culture varies widely throughout the United States; the degree to which it is embraced or denigrated also differs within communities. It offers the potential to bridge home and school communities, and student-parent–teacher age and culture gaps.

Samy Alim (2007), formerly a teacher and now an anthropology professor at UCLA, shows teachers how they can engage students (and, I believe, families) through the pedagogical power of hip-hop culture. *Da Bomb!* was a student-named, student-written literary magazine produced by sixth graders in Philadelphia. Students became "hiphopographers" in order to study the hip-hop culture that was central to many of their lives. They interviewed peers and members of the local hip-hop community, conducted polls, wrote raps and poems, analyzed song lyrics and videos, and wrote biographies of their favorite artists. Alim detailed the goals of *Da Bomb!*:

- To develop skills in writing in several forms and styles— raps, poetry, letters, reviews, short stories, essays, fiction, editorials—and in desktop publishing

- To encourage originality and creativity
- To expose students to multimedia and Internet resources with the aim of developing research skills
- To obtain formal skills in "standard English" writing, speaking, and communicating (p. 21)

How might you use hip-hop pedagogy to engage families? Could students interview their parents about "old school" hip-hop? What if students and families rewrote stories from their reading (either basal readers or classroom library books) setting them in their own neighborhoods and incorporating the language, music, and literacies of their families and friends? An excellent resource is the book and CD *Hip Hop Speaks to Children: A Celebration of Poetry With a Beat* edited by Nikki Giovanni (2008), including artists such as Kanye West, Queen Latifah, Mos Def, and Tupac Shakur along with classic poets such as Langston Hughes and Eloise Greenfield. Families could use raps that students bring home from this collection to compare lyrics of songs dealing with social issues from different eras.

There are many ways to learn about and incorporate family knowledge, languages, and literacies in ways that build bridges between home and school. The critical starting point is believing that this knowledge is valuable to the child's learning.

ACT TO LEARN FROM FAMILY VISITS

At an International Reading Association workshop on family–school partnerships, a wise administrator shared that while all teachers in her school visit regularly with families in their homes and elsewhere, they no longer use the term *home visits*. She explained that some families associated that term with government agencies that might take their children away. They now use the term *family visits* and emphasize working together to support the child, meeting wherever the parents are comfortable.

Isn't it remarkable how something as small as changing a word can change a practice? I'm guessing that someone asked, "Do you have any concerns about my visit to your home?" or "Do you know what we might do so other families would be more comfortable talking with teachers?" Maybe someone just listened more closely to a parent who first declined a home visit by saying, "Well, this is a bad time, the house is a mess." That might mean the parent is uncomfortable with someone coming to her home, in which case another site might be less threatening (see "Arranging the Visit," below); it also might mean that she is wary of the school as a government agency assessing her home and parenting.

How we arrange, interact during, and follow-up on family visits can make the difference between forming a relationship that supports student learning and alienating a parent or caregiver. I hesitate to provide "guidelines," so let's think of these more as starting points for planning family visits. (See online supplementary materials for parents.)

Arranging the Visit

- Explain to the family that you'd like to meet with them so you can get to know each other so you can work together to support their child's learning.
- Arrange a mutually convenient time and place: a chat over coffee in a neighborhood restaurant, parent's workplace, or community center, or a trip to a park where the children can play and adults can talk.
- Determine together who will attend the meeting, welcoming extended family members or an interpreter.
- If possible go in pairs of teachers (e.g., the classroom teacher with the art, PE, ESOL, or reading specialist—the staff who will be working most closely with the child). Schools often recommend going in pairs for safety reasons. You might form these pairs in order to provide translation, to coordinate special services, or to build on a child's strengths and interests.

During the First Visit

- Talk adult to adult, as colleagues—maybe eventually friends—who have this particular child's best interest at heart.
- Rather than going in with a long list of questions, which can be intimidating, simply ask the family to tell you about their child. Follow up by asking, "Tell me about your child as a reader" and "Tell me about your child as a writer."
- Share information about yourself and your interests. Talk about the kinds of literacy activities you do in the

classroom, and why they are important to you as a reader and writer. Invite similar sharing from the family. Let them know you are interested in their work, play, and lives.

- If you are doing family–school journals, newsletters, parent-teacher-student conferences, or family nights, explain how families can be involved to support their children as learners.
- Encourage family members to speak comfortably, in the language they use at home. Spanish, Mandarin, Haitian Creole—the language of the home is the language of learning as a family, whether it is casual conversation about what kids learned at school, writing and reading together, or telling stories.
- Finally, discuss how you can continue conversation throughout the school year—phone calls, face-to-face conversations, or e-mail.

After Each Visit

- Write after each visit. It could be a list of the family's funds of knowledge, ideas for teaching based on this knowledge, or a story of the visit, questions, a poem—write in a form that is comfortable for you. With the family's permission, you may take a few notes during the visit.
- Make time at study group or grade-level meetings to discuss what you learned. What funds of knowledge might you incorporate in the classroom, for example, what texts might students read and write that build on home literacies? How do children learn at home, and how might that translate into literacy instruction?
- Consider how you will use every child's home language as a resource in your classroom.

Overcoming Barriers to Family Visits

There may be many barriers to family visits: some real, some imagined, some based on restrictive school or district policies. There may be issues of time, safety, or comfort from families, teachers, or both. In Gonzáles et al. (2005) teachers usually had multiple visits with only three families. So what are the alternatives for getting to know all families?

Some questions for discussion:

1. What are the barriers for family visits? List each one and then brainstorm how you might overcome each. Draw on the experience of teachers on your faculty or at nearby schools.
2. What are additional places you might form relationships with families? List all the places families in your school might be, such as recreational, religious, eating, and work establishments, flea markets, neighborhood grocery stores, recreation centers, and public library branches.
3. What are additional avenues to learning about families? Think about various technologies, both low and high tech. What role might writing play? How can children help connect teachers and adults in their families?

Continue to learn from families throughout the year. Repeat next year. The neighborhood changes, students change, families change. There will always be new funds of knowledge, new literacies related to popular culture, and new ways language enriches the lives of students at home and at school.

READ TO LEARN MORE

González, N., Moll, L., & Amanti, C. (2005) Funds of knowledge: Theorizing practices in households, communities, and classrooms. Mahwah, NJ: Erlbaum.

> This book explains the theory underlying the funds of knowledge work, research on its impact, and ways that teachers in the original Arizona team and around the country have learned from families and incorporated their funds of knowledge.

McIntyre, E., Kyle, D., Moore, G., Sweazy, R. A., & Greer, S. (2001). Linking home and school through family visits. *Language Arts, 78* (3), 264–272.

> McIntyre and her colleagues explain how they conducted family visits, what they learned, and how the process changed their teaching. They also discuss issues of time, responding to and reporting sensitive information, and the need for emotional support.

CHAPTER 4

Partner Through Photography

When I look at this picture of my child's school, many fond memories came flowing back to me. I remember the first time that I drove Karl to preschool—the excitement, the worries, the anticipation. All day, I couldn't stop thinking about what my child was doing at that very moment, how he would feel about being around other children of his age, and what he'd think of school after that day. That first day is very important because sometimes it can determine if your child will like or dislike that menacing brick building in which he has to spend 8 hours from Monday to Friday. But thankfully, Karl enjoyed his school day very much thanks to the thoughtful teachers and friendly classmates. . . . [T]hat Karl has chosen this out of all the other pictures to write about signifies that he also regards it as being important. . . . Seeing his eager face and the many others at the entrance reminds me how innocence still exists and how the next generation may not be lost after all. (Allen et al., 2002, p. 321)

C ONFERENCES WITH THE parents of Karl, a quiet Chinese third grader, had been challenging for his teacher Cyndy Piha and for the parents because the adults had difficulty understanding each other's language. However, Cyndy noted that entries in the photo journal like this one written by Karl's mother "became a powerful tool for me to make the home/school connection" (p. 321).

In the previous chapter we saw the power of forming relationships with families and learning about their knowledge, languages, and literacies. While personal visits are preferable, they are not always possible with every family. What other ways might we form these relationships to support student learning? One way is through photographs that students and their parents, like Karl's mother, write about.

DISCUSS THE POTENTIAL OF PHOTOGRAPHY

Visual literacy—creating and interpreting visual images such as pictures, art, film, and other media—is often included in elementary curriculum standards. Children encounter the combination of printed text and visual components (illustrations, photographs, visual aids) in many traditional elementary curriculum materials (e.g., library books, textbooks) and nontraditional texts (e.g., graphic novels, Web sites, anime), as well as in their out-of-school experiences with videos, television, billboards, and video games (Fisher & Frey, 2008).

Educators often approach visual literacy as skills students need to read images insightfully and critically. Photography projects such as the one Karl and his family and teacher engaged in put students in the role of creating visual texts. In the PhOLKS project that you'll read about in this chapter, students photographed their out-of-school lives, wrote about the photographs, and invited parents to write about them. This allowed teachers, students, and family member to "see" each other in new ways.

Some questions for discussion:

1. In what ways are families currently involved in your visual literacy curriculum?
2. How can you "picture" using photography to form partnerships with families?

3. What resources do you have as a school to support a photography project (photography expertise among the faculty and families, still or video cameras, software, printers for digital photographs, and so on)?

EXPLORE FAMILY–SCHOOL PARTNERSHIPS THROUGH PHOTOGRAPHY

I was part of a wonderful study group of teachers and teacher educators that explored family funds of knowledge through the lenses of photography and writing. We called ourselves the PhOLKS (Photographs of Local Knowledge Sources) Project. We served a diverse student population (in local terms, Black, Hispanic, White, and international students) primarily in low- or mixed-income urban and rural schools. We valued the multiple perspectives we brought to the study group: African American, Colombian, and European American; Christian and Jewish; male and female; growing up from poor to privileged economically; teaching in special education, English language learner, all-subject classrooms, media centers, and college classrooms. These perspectives helped us understand cultural issues as we shared photographs and the writing from the children and their family members.

Think about your students and their families. How might you adapt this project to learn about their funds of knowledge? (See online supplementary materials for parents.)

PREPARATION FOR PHOTOGRAPHING OUT-OF-SCHOOL LIVES

There are many instructional activities that can help prepare students before they begin taking pictures. These are not "add on" activities; they are ones that can be part of a dynamic reading, writing, and visual literacy curriculum. I encourage you to look at your existing curriculum and see where there are logical connections. Some of the things teachers in the PhOLKS project did to prepare students (Allen et al., 2002) were:

1. Shared photographic essays such as *My Painted House, My Friendly Chicken, and Me* (Angelou, 1994), *Shooting Back from the Reservation: A Photographic View of Life by Native*

American Youth (Hubbard, 1994), and *Daddy and Me: A Photo Story of Arthur Ashe and His Daughter* (Moutoussamy-Ashe, 1993). Media specialists, what do you recommend?

2. Read and discussed books that taught about photography, such as *Click!* (Gibbons, 1997) and *Photography: Take Your Best Shot* (Morgan & Thaler, 1991). Art teachers, what do you recommend?

3. Invited parents who enjoyed photography into the classroom to help children learn how to "see" through the camera's eye.

4. Collaborated with parents. Greg Hull, a pre-K teacher, worked closely with the parents to make picture lists of what their children wanted photographed. Parents then took pictures of what the children chose.

5. Helped students create photographic essays about their lives at school before encouraging them to create similar projects about their lives outside of school.

6. Connected to learning in other parts of the curriculum. Vinette Fabregas's first graders had been reading stories by Patricia McKissack, and enjoyed seeing photographs of her as a child in her life story *Can You Imagine?* (1997). Reading *My Mom Can't See Me* (Alexander, 1990), a selection from a third-grade literature anthology illustrated with photographs, prompted a lively discussion in Cyndy's class about what students might choose to photograph.

7. Brought in some of our own photographs and invited the children and families to share some of theirs.

You could spend a few days or a few weeks at this stage, especially if you connect photography projects to other aspects of your curriculum. For example, Carmen Urdanivia-English created a unit integrating writing, visual literacy, and social studies. She read from her memoir about growing up in Colombia to her fifth-grade English language learners, many of whom came from Mexico. She shared the bilingual book *El Piñatero/The Piñata Maker* by George Ancoña (1994), a Mexican American photographer who documents Mexican history. When students complained that they hated history, Carmen explained, "History is a way of telling people's stories. We can use photography to build history." Students brainstormed how they might use existing and new photographs to "picture" their own histories. Carmen also invited a reporter from the Spanish-language newspaper, *Mexico Lindo*, to show her students ways to document their family and community histories.

Students and Families Writing About Photographs

After all this preparation, students will be eager to take their own pictures. Help students plan what they might photograph: "What is important to you at home? In your neighborhood? What do you and your family like to do together?" Next, determine what cameras you will use, and figure out a rotation for students to take them home. A photography project doesn't have to be expensive. I suggest using digital cameras to avoid processing costs. Some families may have their own digital cameras or cameras on a cell phone, or you can set-up a rotating checkout system for school cameras.

When students have taken their photographs and printed the ones they want to write about, confer with them during writing workshop, asking questions such as "Tell me about this place. Why is it important to you? What is your family doing in this picture? Tell me the story of you and your cousin in this picture." Teachers in the PhOLKS project reported that many students produced more extensive and detailed stories or descriptions of these photographs than they usually wrote. The younger children dictated their narratives. As Vinette pointed out,

> I typed their stories at the classroom computer so they would not get bogged down in the technicalities of writing. This allowed the students to step back and think about the things and people they saw every day. For example, when one boy began to talk about the important things he had photographed like his puppies and his games, he discovered that he had not taken a picture of his grandfather, who had given him these treasured possessions. (Allen et al., 2002, p. 315)

Next we sent the photos home in loose-leaf binders or albums and invited parents or other family members to write about them. Parents contributed detailed descriptions, memories, poetry, letters, and intimate personal stories. Cyndy expressed what many of us felt:

> It was an incredibly moving experience for me to see my kids' lives . . . . It was like going from house to house. . . . I have a very wide

range of children—economically, educationally, ethnically—and every single one of them has a very unique life, a very rich life outside of my classroom, and I forget that. (Allen et al., 2002, p. 315)

Connecting with Families Through Photographs

Photography projects don't stop when the portfolio is complete. They are an opportunity to learn family funds of knowledge and to incorporate them in your literacy teaching practices. For example, if Miguel had not explained it to us, we could only have wondered why he took a picture of an old car seat covered with pine straw in the middle of the woods. Through his photographs and narrations, Miguel articulated his special relationship with his grandparents, who had moved back to El Salvador. He wrote, "This is my *abuelito.* He lived with us a while ago. He found a secret place in the woods. It had seats. He read books there. We found him in his secret place. He said to come in."

Entertainment technology was often a central part of family life. We learned that whole families often watched wrestling together, whereas siblings, cousins, and friends usually played video games like Pokemon and Dragon Ball Z without adults. Fourth-grade teacher Barbara Michalove confessed:

> I tend to be kind of anti TV and video games. . . . But I have had to change my attitude when I see that they are learning things. A lot of kids took pictures of their Nintendo. This is a different kind of play. . . . They have this whole culture around these video games. They will write about something I think is nonsense. All of the other kids right away know what they are talking about. (Allen et al., 2002, p. 315)

Parents helped us see their children as capable learners. Ewa, a Polish newcomer, faced academic and language challenges. Her mother showed us a competent learner:

> This is Ewa's bike. When I look at it I think about the time Ewa learnt to ride a bicycle. . . . Ewa's daddy put a broom stick behind the seat and he was helping her keep balance by holding the stick and running when she was moving. . . . Ewa learnt to ride a two wheeler in three weeks at the age of three years and 9 months, and she wasn't even reaching the ground from the seat. We were all very proud of her. (Allen et al., 2002, p. 315)

Hattie Lawson's third-grade students, predominantly Christian, learned about a classmate's Muslim faith. Najma took the entire roll of film at his mosque so his classmates could "see" inside it. Najma wrote:

> I like this picture because it shows my dad praying in the mosque and some kids pray not just adults. And there's a women's [meeting] room behind the men's [meeting] room, and the men's room is more bigger than the women's room. They pray every day and sometime we eat in the mosque.

Najma wrote a poem in Arabic about a second photo:

> All the names on the wall
> sit on a picture on the wall.
> They sit all day on the wall.
> They never move from the wall.
> They sleep at night all on the wall. (Allen et al., 2002, p. 318)

Hattie added related books to the classroom library and invited Najma's mother to talk with the class. Hattie's students asked enthusiastic questions about what was inside the mosque, what Najma's family did there, and about what it meant to be Muslim. Najma shared how his father read to him twice each night, once from a child's book and once from the Koran. Other children shared photographs portraying family literacies and rituals such as reading Bible stories and saying prayers.

Linda Sprague learned that many of her kindergarteners had a great deal of responsibility at home including meal preparation, caring for younger siblings, and cleaning. The young mother of one struggling student, Demetrious, followed Linda's instructions to photograph her son doing his jobs at home quite conscientiously. This opened up a dialogue between Linda and Mom about concerns they shared about Demetrious. Linda reflected, "I've learned that when parents ask, 'What can I do to help my child in school?' I need to have specific instructions and materials" (Allen et al., 2002, p. 318), like those she provided in the photography project. Once this communication was established, Demetrious made much greater progress, which Linda attributed to his mother working with him at home on the specific things she was teaching at school. Linda also began giving Demetrious and his classmates more responsibility for their own learning, the kind of responsibility they had at home.

ACT TO PARTNER THROUGH PHOTOGRAPHY

How might you design a photography project that helps students and families teach you and each other about their out of school lives?

- What roles will parents play? Will parents help plan the project? Contribute oral, videotaped, or written stories? Plan and participate in an art show at the school, in a neighborhood family center, or at a local art museum?
- What technology will you use—regular, disposable, or digital cameras? Video cameras? Or if you don't have cameras, could students draw important scenes from their lives?
- Will students create photo essays, narratives, poems, or other texts to illuminate each picture? Could they create a verbal narration of a PowerPoint or iMovie presentation?
- And most important, how will you learn together about family funds of knowledge, and how will that support literacy learning in new ways?

I feel certain you will find, as we did, that what you learn has a direct impact on relationships among students, their families, and their teachers that support student learning. Listen to one of those formed in the PhOLKS project:

Cyndy, a White teacher, worried about Kenesha, a Black child who often slept in class, and lived in a trailer with no plumbing and too little food. Other teachers at the school said her mother was never involved; they told Cyndy that the mother had been in special education when she attended the school. Cyndy's contact with the family was Kenesha's aunt, who also intimated that Kenesha's mother was not capable of raising her. Cyndy was delighted to discover what Mom, who had not previously communicated with her, wrote in her daughter's photo journal:

> My daughter name is Kenesha. . . . She stay with her mother that's me. . . . She is very sweet all the teacher and people love her because she

is understanding and nice, polite, sweet, listen, smart. She have her good days & bad days but she is the sweetest child you like to spend time with. She go to church she sings in the choir at church members of the church love to hear her sing she sings so good you love her. She like to read and talk a lot. She loves dogs. She like to play with dolls. She love her new baby brother. (Allen et al., 2002, p. 317)

Cyndy did not ever meet Kenesha's mother, but after this letter, they began communicating frequently by notes and telephone. She wanted to know exactly how Kenesha was doing—"Keep letting me know," she told Cyndy. In turn, she said she would make sure Kenesha got more sleep. One photograph, one invitation to write, and one letter did not change Kenesha's life. The family still struggled, and so did Kenesha. But now there was a team—a teacher at school and mom at home—working together to give Kenesha the best chance of learning possible.

READ TO LEARN MORE

Ewald, W. & Lightfoot, A. (2001). *I wanna take me a picture: Teaching photography and writing*. Boston, MA: Beacon Press.

> This excellent guide to visual literacy is written for parents and teachers. Based on 30 years of experience teaching photography to children, Ewald also emphasizes writing about photographs.

CHAPTER 5

Partner Through Journals

Ms. Shockley: . . . I was so glad for the "homework." It gave me the opportunity to be in the "scholastic" part of [Brandon's] learning. . . . I feel that it has helped Brandon's learning. I remember when the journal first started I would read to Brandon. Towards the end Brandon read to me. He was eager to learn more words so that he could read more, so he learned! I think my child is special. I have only one time to raise him and one time to teach him and one time to be a part of his growing up. If I show I care, then maybe he would be that caring parent also. (Kathryn, quoted in Shockley et al., 1995, p. 27)

RANDON'S MOTHER KATHRYN wrote this letter in the Home Reading Journal in which she, her son, and their teacher corresponded all year.

Not all parents feel this way about what schools ask them to do to support reading at home. Curt Dudley-Marling (2009) and colleagues interviewed 18 African American parents and 14 immigrant parents of English language learners in two urban communities to learn their perceptions of home-school reading practices. Parents identified many efforts the schools made to get their children to read at home: summer book lists, reading incentive or competition programs, book bags sent home with directions for specific activities, and the exhortation to require their children to "just read." To insure the latter, schools required various forms of documentation such as signing reading logs.

Almost all the parents indicated their willingness to do whatever the school asked them to do. However, parents revealed insightful critiques of the ubiquitous "just read" request. Some parents

- were concerned that their children did not enjoy "just read" time, which sometimes became a battle between parent and child;
- didn't see a role for themselves beyond surveillance and documentation;
- were frustrated because when they asked how they could help their children, they were told to just have them read more;
- viewed "just reading" as additional work that actually interfered with required homework, which seemed more important because it was graded.

Dudley-Marling (2009) noted that school officials did not ask parents what kind of help they wanted to support their children's learning, nor did they indicate that they might learn from parents. He concluded that there seemed to be a cultural gap between the family values and expectations and those of the schools and that "a family literacy considerate of the cultural and material lives of families and committed to the academic achievement of all students must seek better understanding of home literacy practices and how to build on those practices in support of school learning."

DISCUSS CURRENT
FAMILY INVOLVEMENT IN READING AND WRITING

Ouch. I think a lot of literacy teachers and teacher educators will feel a jolt reading this critique of "just reading." I suspect many of us have viewed the encouragement to "just read" at home as a low-stress, research-based, enjoyable way to help children become better readers. What else are we asking parents to do to help their children become readers and writers, and how might we find out how our requests are viewed and practiced in families?

Some questions for discussion:

1. What do we ask students to do at home to grow as readers and writers? List all "invitations" and "assignments" at each grade level.
2. What role do we ask parents to take in each? Evaluate the expectations: How well does this practice (a) encourage a love of reading, (b) involve parents in a meaningful way beyond surveillance, (c) "count" as homework, (d) draw on family literacies, and (e) have a reciprocal channel for teaches and parents to talk about concerns, questions, and the child's growth?
3. For whom are these practices working or not working?
4. How can we learn from parents how they view these practices, and their ideas for literacy practices that are consistent with their cultural and family practices?

EXPLORE FAMILY–SCHOOL JOURNALS

There are many ways teachers, students, and families can use journals to dialogue. We'll examine two, Home Reading Journals and Weekend Journals. (See online supplementary materials for parents.)

Home Reading Journals

Betty Shockley (1st grade) and Barbara Michalove (2nd grade) invited families (including Brandon's) to play an important role in their children's literacy development (Shockley et al., 1995) by corresponding in Home Reading Journals. Parents and others in these

African American and European American working-class families sustained a remarkable commitment to read with their children, talk about the books, and write together in the journals 2–3 times a week all year long. One child told Betty, "My mom read . . . while I was taking a bath. Yeah, I was in the tub and she was sitting on the toilet—the lid was down—and reading to me" (p. 20).

Betty and Barbara honored the families' investment of time by responding to every entry during their planning periods. Sometimes it was just a sentence, sometimes two or three, but they always responded before the journal went home again. This was important not only to parents but also to their children. LaToya's mother told Betty, "She comes home with the journal and starts asking me, 'What did she say? What did she say?'" (Shockley et al., p. 20).

At the beginning of first grade, Betty invited families to take an important part in their child's literacy development in this letter on the first page of the journals:

> Homework . . . In our class, reading and writing are viewed as very connected and natural skills to learn. We read many books each day and write like real writers every day. Our homework practices also reflect this style of learning. Each night (except Fridays) your child will bring a book and a reading journal home. Later in the year there will also be some spelling homework. For now, please read WITH your child every night. Remember, your child will be choosing the books s/he takes home, so on occasion the book may be too difficult for your child to read independently. You can help by asking your child if she wants to read the book herself or if she'd rather you read it to her. Then use the journal to write down her responses to the reading. Sometimes YOU may want to write me about the selection yourself and model for your child ways to think about what we read, or sometimes you may want to have your child dictate to you his interpretations, or sometimes your child may want to do it all by himself. What I'm trying to say is, relax—enjoy this time together—there's no one right way. (Shockley et al., 1995, p. 20)

Families took her at her word, establishing their own styles and uses of the journal. They talked about stories, illustrations, information they learned, insights about their children's literacy development, and sometimes the concerns that fill every family's life.

This extended written communication, not about enlisting parents to solve discipline problems or to sign agendas or permission slips, established deep relationships. It also supported emerging readers and writers at home as well as at school in ways neither teacher nor parent could have accomplished alone. Betty and Barbara's "Home Reading Journal Process" is shown in Figure 5.1.

In second grade with most of the same children and families, Barbara Michalove asked parents what their hopes were for the coming school year. Parents decided to continue the Home Reading Journals (but just 2 nights a week) because they valued this opportunity to "do things together," to structure time in their busy lives to interact with their children, and "to communicate with the teacher all the time, not just at conferences" (Shockley et al., p. 25).

Home Reading Journals are places where families can share their literacy practices, as well as express family values. For example, Barbara learned that Debbie often used books to teach her son Adrian moral lessons—a book about an aardvark who got glasses became a lesson on not making fun of people, and Goldilocks reinforced the message that children should listen to their parents. Adrian's parents also expected correct spelling on most words by second grade and had him recopy some of his entries into the journal; Barbara honored this expectation even though she took a more developmental approach to spelling in the classroom.

Mary, LaToya's mom, particularly appreciated books that gave them the opportunity to talk about their African American heritage:

> LaToya read, "Follow the Drinking Gourd." I enjoyed this book with LaToya. I am glad she is finding books to read about her own people. She asked me a lot of questions about slaves and white people and why they hate each other, and why she should be proud to be black. She had so many questions it took us 1 ½ hours to read this book and for me to explain things to her. (Mary, quoted in Shockley et al., 1995, p. 72)

For some families like Pakaysanh's, English was their second language. Families who don't read or write in English (or in any language) can be encouraged to participate by having an English speaker (e.g., older sibling, family friend) read or translate, creating stories from the pictures, having the child read in English and explain the story in her home language, and so on. Early in the year Pakaysanh's father copied parts of the book into the journal. By the

FIGURE 5.1. Home Reading Journal Process

1. Write a letter to parents inviting them to have a regular role in their child's reading and writing development; also explain the project at Open House or during a family visit or some other one-to-one conversation.
2. Explain to students that they will select books to take home with the Home Reading Journal in a ziplock bag to read with someone at home.
3. Determine how many times a week the books and journals will go home.
4. Ask students to identify one or more family members they can read, talk, and write with in the journals.
5. For younger readers, the family member will usually read aloud, then read interactively with the child until s/he is reading independently. If no one at home can read the book, students and parents can "read" the pictures. Older readers may select a section of a chapter book to read and discuss with the family member.
6. Parents (or older siblings, care givers, etc.) write about the book in the journal, based on their conversation with the child. As children become more proficient writers, they take over recording their conversation in the journal. The important aspect is the dialogue about the story!
7. Write a response to each entry. Some teachers do this daily, others create a rotation schedule. It should not take more than 1 minute per journal in most cases.
8. Simply write "No Response" and the date if there is none; keep sending it home.
9. Keep the focus on enjoying reading and talking about books, and how to help the child grow as a reader and writer. This is not the place to discuss behavior, lunch money, or homework—except this homework!

middle of first grade Pakaysanh did almost all the writing, but he also reported that he often read the books to his parents.

Journals often became a site of collaborative literacy support. Parents suggested that teachers send home books that were harder, or easier, or had more words. Teachers suggested that parents try reading a difficult book to the child first, then listening to the child read. They discussed complexities such as the difficulty of comprehending when the child was spending so much energy on decoding. Many parents had not completed high school, but shared thoughtful insights because they were invited into a genuine dialogue where teachers respected their opinions and often followed their suggestions.

For example, Janice read with Lakendra nearly every night throughout first and second grade. She observed her daughter's reading and asked questions in the journal. The following excerpt from an ongoing exchange concerning comprehension illustrates that she was a keen observer, and that she saw Barbara and herself as a teaching team:

> *Janice*: [Lakendra] read the words real good but it is so hard for her to tell me what she read. I really don't know what to do now. If you have any suggestions of what I can do next I am willing to listen.
> *Barbara*: Maybe try reading her stories and then discussing them together. Perhaps she is concentrating so hard on reading the words that she can't comprehend the whole story. Let me know if this helps—Thanks for being concerned and helping Lakendra! (Shockley et al., 1995, p. 44)

Parents and teachers supported each other as equal teachers of the child. They encouraged, thanked, empathized, problem-solved, consoled, and celebrated. For example, Janice wrote at the end of one entry, "Thanks for yal great methods of teaching." In turn, the teachers often encouraged parents, as when Barbara wrote, "Janice, Lakendra is doing well with reading and writing in class too. Thanks for taking the time to listen to her read. It really makes a difference" (Shockley et al., 1995, p. 46).

Weekend Journals

Andrea Neher (2009), a first-grade teacher in a Title 1 school, felt she communicated well with parents. Her students, African American and recent immigrants from Mexico, El Salvador, and Costa Rica, took home a daily agenda with notes reminding students and parents of homework, field trips, and short notes celebrating learning, for example, when their child wrote a thoughtful piece during writing workshop.

When she joined a study group focused on family–school partnerships that support learning, Andrea decided that one-way communication with parents was not enough. The group read about Home Reading Journals in *Creating Welcoming Schools* (Allen, 2007) and Weekend Journals in *Parents and Teachers Working Together* (Davis & Yang, 2005). Struck by the potential of two-way communication with parents about what students were learning each week, Andrea wrote the following letter, incorporating advice from Davis and Yang:

Dear Parents,

The children and I have an exciting new project to share with you: the Weekend Family Journal. Each Friday, your child will bring home a letter s/he wrote to you, telling one thing about that week at school. Please read each week's message and ask your child to tell you about the message and any drawing with it. Don't worry if the message is difficult to read—it is written by your first-grader's spelling ☺ Your child's messages will become easier to read as the year progresses.

Please write a message back to your child each week in the notebook right after your child's message. Anyone at home is welcome to write back—a parent, a sibling, or another relative, or a family friend. The message may be written in English, Spanish, or both languages. The important thing is that your child receives a reply. When your child brings the journal back to school, I will write a message to both you and your child that you can read together the next time the journal goes home.

To keep this project working smoothly, please

- Write about the same topic as your child.
- Use print, not cursive, writing.
- Have your child read your message over with you.
- Send the journal back with your child each Monday.
  Your child may share your message with the class.

The at-home part of this project should take no more than 10 or 15 minutes. This short routine, done each week, can be so helpful to your child's learning. Thank you for partnering with your child in this important work!

Please let me know if you have any questions.

Sincerely, Mrs. Neher

Andrea glued this letter inside each child's Weekend Family Journal, a hard-back sewn composition book tough enough for the ins and outs of backpack routines. The school's bilingual Family Engagement Specialist translated the letter and subsequent correspondence into Spanish for Andrea's Latino families, and into English when parents responded in Spanish.

Students were excited about the project. One student asked, "Mrs. Neher, can I write in Spanish? My mom don't speak English." Andrea suggested they write the note in English first since that was the language they wrote in at school, and then write it in Spanish. This proved difficult in a school with no focus on biliteracy. Once again, Andrea turned to the Family Engagement Specialist, who agreed to translate the children's short messages into Spanish. In a school without a bilingual liaison, one in which multiple languages are spoken in homes, or one where many teachers needed weekly translation, teachers might draw on family networks. Asking students, "Who do you know who could translate this for you?" is a critical part of successful weekend journals.

Each Friday during writers workshop, Andrea's class discussed what they had learned that week—an important way for a teacher to find out what stands out for students from their teaching! During the first few weeks, Andrea guided the class in crafting a letter through shared writing. They discussed what they would tell about their learning that week, and what question to ask their family member related to that learning. Andrea wrote the group construction on a chart for each to copy into his or her journal (later in the year students wrote their own highlights and questions). For example, after a field trip where students learned about solar energy, they wrote about the trip and asked parents how they were saving energy at home. One parent responded:

> You asked me how we save electricity at home. Funny you should ask that. Our bill is the highest it's ever been so since it's cooler outside I've been cutting the air off at night and raising the windows . . . you have been helping me by not running in and out the front door and by keeping the lights off. Thank you. Your Mama. (Neher, 2009, n.p.)

Parents or some adult responded to the question in the journal over the weekend, and the students read aloud their responses during Monday's Morning Meeting, bringing family voices and experiences into the learning process. Andrea wrote back to both students and parents during the week, and on Friday the cycle began again.

Home Reading Journals and Weekend Journals are just two of many possibilities for ongoing, two-way communication that support literacy learning. What makes sense for teachers, families, and students in your grade level at your school?

ACT TO PARTNER THROUGH JOURNALS

In an interview Stephen Covey was asked, "Should parents help with homework?" He replied, "Have your kids teach you what they're learning [in school]. Get excited and enthusiastic so kids start to yell, 'Wow, my parents are really learning. I'm their teacher. I'm a good student'" (McDowell, 2009, p. 24). Research tells us that one of the most important things parents can do to support their children's learning is to talk with them about what they are studying, to use academic language, and to connect school learning and home learning.

In partnering with families through journals, remind yourself to keep the focus on encouraging literacy and learning-related conversations at home. Here are three starting points, in order of the time commitment required:

1. Create an interactive classroom newsletter, learning folder response area, or other forum related to what you are already sending home. Each Friday, Molly Rose (whom we met in Chapter 2) sent home a one-page Rose Room Letter with information for parents about field trips, and so on. What made Molly's newsletter unique was the "Ask Me . . . " section, 10–12 questions parents or other family members could ask children about their learning that week. In addition, on each student's envelope of work from the week, Molly wrote a note about the child as a learner on one side, and space for parents to respond (Lawrence-Lightfoot, 2003). What are you sending home related to your students' learning? How can you prompt family conversation about the content and/or two-way communication between parents and teacher?
2. Start some kind of weekly journal such as Weekend Journals (Davis & Yang, 2005) or Family Message Journals (Wollman-Bonilla, 2000). Family Message Journals, unlike others discussed in this chapter, are a written dialogue between students and families, without teacher response.

Students write about what they are learning and parents respond; their responses then become part of the classroom curricular discussions when students read them aloud. Both these options require less teacher time than Home Reading Journals.

3. Start Home Reading Journals. Yes, this one is the most time consuming. It may also be the most directly related to your students' development as readers and writers. You can manage the time by staggering your responses, maybe 10 a day.

READ TO LEARN MORE

Shockley, B., Michalove, B., & Allen, J. (1995). *Engaging families: Connecting home and school literacy communities*. Portsmouth, NH: Heinemann.

This book includes all the details of Home Reading Journals, "Tell me about your child," and other family–school parallel practices, plus three family portraits showing dialogue and growth over 2 years.

Wollman-Bonilla, J. (2000). *Family message journals: Teaching writing through family involvement*. Urbana, IL: National Council of Teachers of English.

Wollman-Bonilla provides all the details of implementing these learning-focused journals, as well as documentation of student growth as writers during the year.

CHAPTER 6

Invite Family Voices
Into Literacy Practices

Mommy, where did you meet Daddy?
    Well, your Dad and I were both in the Army in 1979. We were
both stationed at Fort Polk, Louisiana.
Yeah, that's where Mrs. Barbara and Mr. Hank live.
    We became good friends. After a year . . . we decided to get mar-
ried and all of the wedding plans were made. . . . Then one week before
the wedding we were sent on a secret mission—yeah, really secret. We
couldn't tell anyone. I could only tell Grandmom we were leaving and
we would miss the wedding. (Debbie and Adrian Anderson, quoted in
Schockley et al., 1995, p. 38)

W HEN TEACHER BETTY SHOCKLEY invited her student and his mom to write a family story, they wrote the dialogue story quoted above. In it Adrian learns of his parents' secret mission with refugees from Cuba, how his parents were stationed in Germany, and where in their many moves Adrian was born. Debbie adopted the format of *Tell Me a Story, Mama* (Johnson, 1989) about an African American family like theirs; she and Adrian had enjoyed reading it during their Home Reading Journal time.

How do teachers invite families to connect to their children's school literacy lives? In this chapter we'll explore further that key finding from Henderson and Mapp (2002): Programs and interventions that *engage families in supporting their children's learning at home* are linked to improved student achievement.

DISCUSS YOUR CLASSROOM LITERACY STRUCTURES

In Chapter 5 you evaluated the invitations and assignments you send home to families, and how they respond. Now let's discuss what you do in your daily literacy practices that families could also participate in.

1. What are the literacy routines that are most important in your classroom? These might be writing workshop, independent reading, writing responses to literature, guided reading, literature circles, reading aloud and so on.
2. What ways might parents and families be involved in one or more of these literacy routines? For example, Home Reading Journals (Chapter 5) involve parents directly in their children's independent reading at home.

EXPLORE INVITATIONS TO
EXTEND CLASSROOM LITERACY STRUCTURES

Inviting Families Into Writing Workshop

Educators and children's book authors Alma Flor Ada and Isabel Campoy (2004) work with teachers to create writing communities "in which equality, justice and peace are explored in both thought and action" (p. 4). Teachers write and then invite children and family members to author poems, stories, photo essays, and books. They write on themes such as Recognizing Human Qualities, Building Communities, and Understanding the Past, Creating the Future. These themes become central to both schoolwork and homework.

If you invited family members to be part of your writing program, what might it look like? We know parents and caregivers can't come in for writing workshop everyday, but Ada and Campoy have created ways that family voices can become a part of the classroom through their writing and creating at home. They give a basic pattern for the authoring process (Ada & Campoy, 2004, pp. 6–7), which I've extended with ways to build on family funds of knowledge, language, and literacies (in italics).

1. Teacher and students discuss high-quality children's literature on the theme.
    Students and families can also gather and contribute texts from their home and community—news articles, song lyrics, paintings, comic books, poetry, picture books, Internet sites.
2. Students share the texts with families and discuss the theme.
    Invite families to share their perspectives on the theme through student interviews or in a home reading journal or weekend journal (Chapter 5).
3. Students and teacher talk about the theme of the unit.
    Students will read from their interviews or the journals parents wrote, bringing family perspectives into the discussion and bringing in conversation from home related to the theme.
4. Students and teacher select one text for Creative Literacy Dialogue. This deep comprehension approach starts with description and personal interpretation of the text, then moves to high-order critical, multicultural, and antibias perspectives, and culminates in the creative transformative action phase (see Figure 6.1).
    With the many specific texts and questions Ada and Campoy provide as examples, teachers and students can generate great questions to ask parents or other family members in dialogue journals or as a homework assignment.
5. The teacher writes his or her own book or poem, and then shares it with students who take a copy home to share with their families.
6. Students and families create their own poems, photo essays, books, and so on. Teachers encourage family members to write in their home language, and if they are not comfortable writing, to tell their children what they

FIGURE 6.1. Example of Ada and Campoy's Creative Literacy Process

Unit 4: Building Communities, Questions to Initiate the Dialogue

1. Read the bilingual poetic ABC book *Gathering the Sun* (Ada, 2001), which celebrates migrant farmworkers.
2. *Descriptive phase:* Questions to develop an understanding of the message of the book.
    a. What have you learned about the life of the Mexican farmworkers in the United States that you did not know before?
    b. What is you favorite poem in the book? Why?
3. *Personal interpretive phase:* Questions to encourage the expression of feelings and emotions in response to the book and to relate the book's content to the reader's experiences.
    a. What do you know about the life of your parents and your grandparents when they were children? What would you like to know?
    b. What are some of the things you feel proud about with regard to your own family, community, and culture?
4. *Critical, multicultural, antibias phase:* Questions to promote higher thinking skills and to encourage reflection on the themes of equality, inclusion, respect, justice, and peace.
    a. Many children of migrant farmworkers have grown up without ever having had a home of their own, and having had to change schools several times a year. Why would this be hard on you? What are your thoughts about this?
    b. Part of the reason why migrant farmworkers are mistreated is that they belong to a different origin and culture than the people in power. Can you think of other cases in which the people's differences have been used to oppress them?
5. *Creative transformative phase:* Questions to lead to creative, constructive action that encourages understanding and respect for others and to become more responsible for bringing about positive change in our own reality.
    a. What things do we have in common with farmworkers? With all other human beings?
    b. What can we do to help others who are not being treated fairly?

Note. From *Authors in the Classroom: A Transformative Education Process* (p. 123), by A. Ada and I. Campoy, 2004, New York: Allyn & Bacon.

want to say so the children can write it down. *Adults in the family could also tape-record the story, proverb, or advice, literally bringing parent's voices into the classroom.*
7. Share the products. Teachers often create classroom books with contributions from all children and families. Many books are written in the families' home languages and also translated into English.
8. Celebrate together. Family events are profoundly moving and educational, as participants reflect on their learning processes and beautiful literary products.

Inviting Families Into Read-Alouds: "Must-Read" Texts

Teacher researcher Alfred Tatum (2005) was concerned when several of his Black male students did not seem engaged during reading. These were middle schoolers, but I'll bet some of you teaching intermediate grades have similar concerns about students who say they hate to read, can't read, or are "bored" by reading. One successful strategy Tatum developed to engage his students was introducing them to high interest "must-read" texts rather than trying to cajole them into reading "have-to-read" texts in a mandated curriculum.

For Tatum's students, must-read texts were ones of critical important to a young Black male's identity and development such as *The Autobiography of Malcolm X* (1965), books by Walter Dean Myers, and *A Raisin in the Sun* by Lorraine Hansberry (1971). You may be thinking, what must-read texts are there for my young girls from Mexico, my Hmong kindergarteners, my students living in poverty? What are the texts that will empower them, allow them to see their cultural experiences represented in print, challenge them to aspire to achieve as writers, artists, or scientists? And how in the world am I going to find these texts for the wealth of diverse readers (and nonreaders) I teach?

Here's my answer: Parents. Grandparents. Older siblings. Community members. There are people in children's lives who could recommend must-read texts. These may be magazine articles, poems, books, newspaper articles they've saved, song lyrics, movie dialogue, or plays. Tatum pointed out that the Internet makes access to such texts easier. How can we gather this information from family members? I'll offer two possibilities and leave it to you to come up with others.

Student Survey. Develop a short survey with your students. Help them brainstorm a list of people they will ask to respond. Questions might include something like the following (but they'll be much more meaningful if the kids generate the language):

1. What is the most important thing you ever read? Why?
2. Is there a book (or poem or news story) that influenced you to be the person you are today? How?
3. Is there something that you read when you were my age that influenced how you think of yourself as [a Puerto Rican woman, a Korean-American man, an African American community leader]?
4. Do you have any "must-read" items (newspaper clippings, magazine articles, poems, books) that I could take into my classroom? Would you be able to come visit my classroom to talk about why a piece of writing was so important to you?

Family Reading or Literacy Night. Many teachers I've talked with find Family Reading Night more valuable when families gather in their child's classroom. Families can get to know each other, and teachers and families can deepen their relationships. For families with more than one child in the school, family members could split up (encourage older siblings and other relatives to attend), or families might alternate. This is a real concern, so do talk with families to figure this out. I speak as a mom who had three children in elementary school at one time!

You might plan two paired Family Reading Nights that focus on must-read texts. The first Family Reading Night might be a sharing of must-reads generated by the survey. Invite families to bring in one or more must-read texts. Form a circle in the classroom, or divide into two or more smaller circles. Invite adults to share their reading in any way that they are comfortable—reading their favorite part, telling about why the piece is important to them, or both. Give time for others to respond and make connections.

At a second Family Reading Night, bring in a wide range of contemporary and classic children's literature, poems, children's magazine articles, and other texts that reflect the cultural heritages of families—all families—in your classroom. Enlist the help of your students, school media specialist (who may have great film recommendations too), and teachers who know multicultural children's literature and popular culture. For example, comic books were important to many people in my generation; graphic novels, anime, and other texts hook readers in my grandchildren's generation.

When families gather, have the texts spread out all over the room. As you greet people, hand them some sticky notes and pencils. Invite them to browse through all the texts and mark "Must-Read" and their name on any they think should be part of your curriculum in the coming months. Kids can read to their families and lobby for their favorites. Explain that some of these you will read aloud, some will be available for students to bring home and read with their families, and some will be read by students in literature circles or during their daily independent reading time. This gives you a good opportunity to demonstrate all the times kids read in your classroom.

What are *your* must-read books, graphic novels, or poems? Teachers deepen the family-classroom partnership when they share something personal on Family Reading Night. Bring in a must-read book or other text from your childhood that helped shape who you are as a woman or man, how you view your race or ethnicity, how you think about your language, religion, or sense of place.

Now for the most important part—students and families reading must-read texts aloud together at home. Invite this reading, discussion, and writing in Home Reading Journals or as a homework assignment. Students can read what they and their parents wrote about the text during sharing, create a bulletin board with favorite quotes, or take over the daily read-aloud time one day a week with must-read excerpts.

Inviting Families Into Poetry Projects

I love reading and writing poetry and teach a class on the many ways poetry enriches the elementary curriculum. Let me share a few snapshots of poetry projects that might inspire you to plan your own, with families of course.

Capturing a Community. Andy Plemmons (2006) involved his third-grade students and their families in an exploration of historical places in their rural Georgia community.

1. Students asked their parents about covered bridges, old mills, schools, and other historic sites. Andy reported that this created a "dynamic dialogue between students and

parents. . . . Parents were able to share what they knew . . . and to tell childhood stories of the way things used to be" (p. 84).

2. Andy taught some basics about photography, then students took home disposable cameras. With their parents they photographed their chosen historic site.

3. In addition to gathering parent stories about sites, students researched them on the Internet, and parents and other guest speakers came to talk about historic preservation of these community sites.

4. Andy taught a series of minilessons using mentor poems in writing workshop. Students wrote, incorporated their research, revised, shared, and published their photographs and poems.

5. Parents came to the Poetry Reading—and beamed with pride. Each family then selected a place in the community to deliver a copy of the book. Students were thrilled when they received letters from people who had read their poetry at the courthouse, a bed and breakfast, and the historical society.

This is my favorite poem by one of Andy's students (Plemmons, 2006, p. 109):

The Old School House is Waiting,
by Colton Lowder

I am the old school house
My metal roof
And broken windows
Shine in the light
My doors are waiting
Until the day
That children
Once again
Walk through
Please restore me
Please don't move me
Let me once again
Hear the cry of
RECESS!

"Where I'm From" and "I Am" Poems. Many teachers across grade levels throughout the country use George Ella Lyons' poem "Where I'm From" as a catalyst and "mentor poem" for young poets. Lyons (1999) suggests an adaptable process for writing "Where I'm From" poems. Terry Nestor, a second-grade teacher in Athens, Georgia, guides her diverse group of students in writing their own versions, drawing on conversations with their families about meaningful people, sayings, and places. They then write "We Are From" compilation poems to highlight both the diversity and the commonalities of the classroom community, as in the following excerpt: "We are from Georgia, Atlanta, Miami, Jacksonville, California, Holland, Madison County, Utah, Pittsburgh, Washington, Jamaica, China, and the Planet Earth."

Some teachers extend the invitation to families after students have written their poems. Sixth-grade teacher Maria del Rosario Barillas taught in a Latino neighborhood in southern California. Using a patterned poem framework (I am . . . I wonder . . . I feel . . .) supported both students and their parents. Students wrote their own "I Am" poems and shared them with families. Barillas then invited parents to write a poem using the same pattern. One mother wrote in Spanish,

> I want my children to study to have a better future.
> I feel happiness and pride when my son earns certificates.
> I touch the minds of my children so that they can understand
>   and learn.
> I worry that my son will find friends that will take him on a
>   path away from his studies. (quoted in Barillas, 2000, p. 307)

Songs are often an excellent way to draw in students who might be turned off to other forms of poetry. You and your students can probably think of several songs that have the basic theme of "this is who I am, where I'm from," for example, "We Are Family" (Sister Sledge), "I Am Woman" (Helen Reddy), and "Where I'm From" (Digable Planets). How can you build on student and family interest in music? (See online supplementary materials for parents.)

1. Ask students to bring in recordings and lyrics of songs they relate to after sharing several "I Am" poems. Bring in some of your own.

2. Help students pick a "theme song"—one that "tells us something about who you are, what's important to you, where you are from."
3. Prepare students to share their projects with family members, and ask parents, grandparents, and others who are important to them to share their own "theme song." Students and families together can write the lyrics and the story of each person's theme song.
4. Collaborate with families on a final project. These might include CD covers, photo stories with the music, a class "We Are Family" CD, and sharing songs on a class website or social networking page.

ACT TO DEVELOP HOME–CLASSROOM LITERACY PARTNERSHIPS

Jim Cummins (1989) noted that a sense of alienation is a major source of school failure. He stressed that a genuine partnership between teachers and parents validates and incorporates family language and cultural perspectives. This is especially true for children and families who are not part of the dominant culture portrayed in many school texts and materials. When families are invited to join their children and teachers as storytellers and writers, their voices fill the classroom even when they are not physically present. How will you act to bring those voices into the classroom?

Having open lines of communication is vital. These concerns can lead to actions:

1. What are the literacy routines that are most important in your classroom? Select just one literacy routine where you would most like to involve families.
2. Initiate a conversation with parents at Open House, conferences, family visits, or by phone. Tell them about what you do in the classroom during the literacy routine you've selected and invite them to ask their child about it and to visit if they are able.
3. Brainstorm and problem-solve together. How might they participate in a meaningful way at home in writing workshop, reading must-read texts, writing poetry, or whatever you've selected? What are the difficulties parents see given family structure, routines, and priorities?

What adults (and even older youth) might be involved? What different roles might they take (listening to a child read, writing a family story, helping a writer revise)? For example, Tizard, Schofield, and Hewison (1982) found that 6- to 8-year-old children in working-class neighborhoods who struggled in school benefited significantly from reading to their parents, even when the parents were not strong readers. In fact, they benefited more from this practice than from additional school instruction from a reading specialist. We can reassure parents that their role is an important one.

READ TO LEARN MORE

McCaleb, S. P. (1997). *Building communities of learners: A collaboration among teachers, students, families, and community.* Mahwah, NJ: Erlbaum.

Extensive processes for structuring family stories around broad topics such as Our Family History, The Wise Ones, and A Book for Peace; includes many examples of both student and parent writing.

Ada, A. F., & Campoy, I. (2004). *Authors in the classroom: A transformative education process.* New York: Allyn & Bacon.

Includes rationale, process, and 10 units with a wealth of examples written by teachers, students, and parents.

CHAPTER 7

Engage Families in Critical Literacy Inquiry

DENISE, A FOURTH GRADER who used a combination of a hearing aid and lip reading to communicate, was from a deaf family. After interviewing her mother for a class study on discrimination, Denise wrote this account:

> My mom could not order the food through the speaker at McDonalds. So she went through the drive in and tried to order the food through writing on a piece of paper. But the person at the window would not take the order. That person told my mom to go inside of McDonalds and order the food. (Michalove, 1999, p. 29)

Denise's classmates were outraged at someone being denied equal access at McDonalds. And yet these same students often denied Denise and several other classmates access to playground games, reading invitations, and other peer-selected events (as I'll describe later in this chapter). Denise's mother told this story because Barbara Michalove invited families to be an integral part of a critical inquiry on prejudice. Her words and those of other parents became an important part of the classroom text for this inquiry.

What is a *critical inquiry*? Critical educators encourage students to question the world, including the texts they read and view. They teach students how to examine inequities in society and work toward meaningful change through their writing. Do we dare to become critical literacy educators? Do we dare invite parents to join in critical inquiries? Do we dare not to?

DISCUSS HOW FAMILIES PARTICIPATE IN CRITICAL LITERACY INQUIRIES

Maria Sweeney, a fourth-grade teacher in suburban New Jersey, challenged her students to confront inequities and work toward a more just and democratic society by teaching them to consider alternative viewpoints in the texts they read and wrote. She taught her students to ask questions of all kinds of texts—children's literature, events they observed, various media, and textbooks (Sweeney, 1999, p. 97):

- Is this fair?
- Is this right?
- Does this hurt anyone?
- Is this the whole story?
- Who benefits and who suffers?
- Why is it like this?
- How could it be different, more just?

Teachers like Maria who take a critical literacy perspective encourage students to go beyond the words on the page (or the television, news program, or YouTube video). As students read, view, or write texts, critical educators equip them to question and evaluate, pushing toward the highest levels of comprehension. Students discuss power structures related to issues that directly affect them, their families, and their communities: race, social class, gender, language, religion, family structures, ability, and many other cultural influences. As you can imagine, involving families is particularly important in such inquiries.

As you talk with colleagues about the ideas in this chapter, think about where you stand and where you might be inviting parents to stand. Perhaps you are just starting to think about helping your students become critical readers and writers. Perhaps your entire year is organized around critical literacy like teachers Mary Cowhey (2006) or Vivian Vasquez (see Critical Literacy in Practice podcasts at http://www.clippodcast.com). Or are you somewhere in the middle of this continuum: You have many legitimate questions about taking on social issues through discussing children's literature, studying issues in the community, and writing for social change. Further, you might be wondering how families figure into your deliberations.

Some questions for discussion:

1. As you plan critical literacy book discussions, inquiry units, or an entire curriculum, how do you bring in the multiple viewpoints, experiences, and beliefs of families?
2. How has your school engaged families in sensitive issues in the past, for example, book selection (or banning) or discussions of volatile local or national events?
3. How might you engage families in critical literacy inquiries in ways that bring in multiple perspectives, diffuse criticism, and enrich the inquiry?

EXPLORE HOW TEACHERS INVITE FAMILIES INTO CRITICAL LITERACY INQUIRIES

Studying Prejudice in History and Ourselves

Barbara Michalove (1999) taught 25 fourth graders in a Title 1 school in a predominantly African American neighborhood. She was disturbed when she heard some of her students name-calling and excluding two Hispanic students who were new to the neighborhood; some also treated two students with hearing impairments negatively. "I realized we had to address the problem directly," Barbara said. "Discussing a children's book about how one kind of animal didn't like another kind wasn't going to cut it" (p. 24). She designed an integrated language arts/social studies unit: Studying Prejudice in History and in Ourselves. Here are some of the major components of how students and their families studied prejudice:

1. Students read and discussed biographies of many people who overcame prejudice, including Marian Anderson, Roberto Clemente, Mae Jemison, and Albert Einstein.
2. Barbara read aloud historical fiction dealing with prejudice, including *Letters from Rifka* (Hesse, 1994), *Reflections of a Black Cowboy* (Miller, 1991), and *The Friendship* (Taylor, 1987).
3. Students recorded and discussed new vocabulary: *discriminate, prejudice, bigotry, sexism, biased, racism, attacker, racist, intolerance, stereotype,* and *victim;* throughout the study they added examples from their readings to each word.
4. Students generated a list of why they thought some people discriminated, including "the way they were raised," "fear," "religion," and "to feel powerful."
5. Students and their families found examples of prejudice in the newspaper and brought these in for class discussions.
6. Students viewed segments of *The Shadow of Hate: A History of Intolerance in America* (Guggenheim, 1995) and convinced Barbara to show the whole video; they expressed great indignation at the many examples of discrimination.
7. Students interviewed family members, asking if they had ever been discriminated against. Parents or students wrote their family stories; students shared these and added family members' names to the examples list under *racism, sexism,* and so on.
8. Some, but not all, students wrote about times they had felt discriminated against; for some it was too big a risk.

To bring the inquiry back to the classroom, Barbara read *Amazing Grace* (Hoffman, 1991). Classmates tell Grace that she can't star in Peter Pan because she is Black and a girl. When Barbara asked, "Does anything like this ever happen in our class?" the floodgates opened, and the children recounted many examples of their own prejudicial words and actions. After much discussion, they generated a list of six positive guidelines for their classroom, including "Treat others the way you want to be treated" and "Put a note on their desk to remind them to be kind." Students began to treat each other differently, and parents noticed. Barbara wrote,

> At parent conferences several weeks later, unsolicited, one black parent and one white parent (whose child had been teased considerably less about his weight since our discussions) told me how much they appreciated the study. They said that their children were really more aware of the issues now, and the adults appreciated the opportunity to talk with their children about such concerns at home, to be resources for their child's schoolwork. (Michalove, 1999, p. 31)

Reading and Writing for a Better World

Many elementary teachers tell me that persuasive writing is a particularly difficult mode to teach. What can be done after reading *Don't Let the Pigeon Drive the Bus* (Willems, 2003) and *Click, Clack, Moo* (Cronin, 2005), delightful but limited persuasive text models? The problem may lie in teaching this mode according to a schedule rather than grounding persuasive writing in children's lives, passions, and local issues that demand writing for specific action.

Randy and Katherine Bomer (2001) suggest making parents and other community members part of a process of "collaborating on texts for public purposes." (See online supplementary materials for parents.) In Katherine's elementary classroom, writing for social action was central to learning. The following process is fluid and adaptable, and could include families at key points (in italics). Students can

- Look periodically through their writing notebooks for social issues that are important in their lives.
- Discuss these entries with partners during morning meeting.
- *Ask at home, "What social or political issues are important to our family?"* In Katherine's New York City classroom, issues included school uniforms, city ordinances, and "keeping real estate out of the hands of developers" (Bomer & Bomer, p. 125).

- Collect articles from newspapers and other sources reflecting differing views related to their topics. *Parents can help students collect information and viewpoints by sharing their life experiences, guiding online searches at home or the library, taking children to local events to hear speakers or participate in rallies, and helping children find print, television, and other media on their issue.*

- Invite parents and community members into the classroom to talk about how they have been involved in working for social change. In Katherine's classrooms various family and community members over the years talked about being arrested in a protest rally, raising money for Doctors Without Borders, and circulating petitions protesting high-stakes testing.

- Create coalitions: students present their issue on posters to interest others and form inquiry teams. *Parents can help design the posters.*

- Participate in teacher-led minilessons, for example, on reading critically for multiple perspectives, creating a powerful name for the inquiry group, organizing and storing information, and working together in groups.

- Learn from critical mentor texts. These might include biographies of change agents, social issue picture books, articles in magazines and newspapers, and primary sources, especially the writings and speeches of social activists. One of my favorite books is *Ten Amazing People and How They Changed the World* (Shaw, 2002). Shaw includes quotes, timelines, and expository writing to share the lives and deeds of activists including Black Elk, Thich Nhat Hanh, Mother Theresa, Malcolm X, and Dorothy Day. *Parents can help identify texts.*

- Study examples of "writing that changed the world" (Bomer & Bomer, 2001, p. 128); Katherine's students analyzed a Rachel Carson essay about the environment, some of Martin Luther King's speeches, poems by poets such as Walt Whitman and Adrienne Rich, song lyrics from various social movements, and excerpts from Stowe's *Uncle Tom's Cabin*. Students detailed strategies these writers used to persuade specific audiences. *Family members can be especially helpful in identifying songs that influenced them on social issues, as well as other kinds of persuasive texts—speeches, sermons, political debates, editorials,*

*and so on. Some family members may come into the classroom
to share music or other texts and why that text was persuasive
to them during social movements such as civil rights for women,
African Americans, immigrants, or gay and lesbian families.*

- Develop action plans. This phase includes extensive
  writing (and revision) of persuasive texts such as petitions,
  posters, news releases, and letters to people in positions
  of power. Katherine focused writing minilessons and
  conferences on considering audience, clarifying purpose,
  including relevant statistics, citing authorities, and other
  evidence to persuade. Students studied examples from *The
  Kids' Guide to Social Action* (Lewis, 1998). *Homework during
  this phase could include reading drafts and getting feedback from
  friends and family with different positions on the issues and of
  different ages.*

- Take action—circulate the petition, send the letters, share
  the posters. Not all letters to the editor will be published,
  not all people in power will write back, but perhaps
  enough will. Perhaps some policy or practice will change.
  Parents and teachers can help students be prepared and resilient.

- Reflect and evaluate the process. *Family members can help
  students think and write about what they learned, what they
  accomplished, their disappointments, and most importantly what
  their next steps might be in writing to change the world.*

Inquiries Initiated at Home

Art teacher Patty Bode had a message box in her classroom. She
had the following exchange with a first grader:

Dear !!!!!! mis Boudie

Ples! halp. my moom was spcing to me abut wite piple leving
bran and blak piple out of books. Love Kaeli

Dear Kaeli,

Today I found your note in my message box. I was very interested
to hear that you were speaking to your mom about White people leaving Brown and Black people out of books. I am glad you asked for
help.

This is a problem that we need to help each other with. We need
to ask our friends and teachers and families for help so we can work
together.

I think we should work on this problem in art class. Maybe our class could design our own books which include all kinds of people of all colors, races, and all families. Maybe we could write some letters to book publishers and send them our artwork to give them some good ideas for improving their books.

See you in art class! Love, Ms. Bode (Nieto, 1999, p. 125)

Ms. Bode read Kaeli's letter to the class. Kaeli showed the book that had prompted the letter, a book about the human body with hundreds of pictures. Kaeli found only 22 people of color. This sparked an extended inquiry that involved the following:

- Discussing vocabulary related to race and ethnicity (e.g., *White* or *European American*) and discrimination (e.g., *fair, stereotype*)
- Analyzing children's books for fair representation,
- Learning color theory, studying skin tones, creating artwork of students' faces
- Taking direct action by writing letters and sending their artwork to publishers (Nieto, 1999, pp. 125–129)

I love how a literacy event at home sparked an in-depth critical inquiry in the classroom. Talk about building curriculum on genuine questions! Patty Bode got me thinking about all the possibilities for families to be involved in such an inquiry. What if students asked their parents to help them do these things:

- Keep a log at home for one week of pictures in every book, magazine, or newspaper article anyone in the family reads. Analyze who is missing, who is represented, and how. Teachers and students could keep a class log that included textbooks, classroom read-alouds, library books, and so on. To extend this critical media literacy, families might similarly analyze television shows, movies, videogames, or YouTube videos the following week.
- Survey friends and family members about how they refer to themselves and others in terms of racial or ethnic identity. This may lead to deeper family inquiry about how terms have evolved historically and in their own families, and the political roots and implications of, for example, *Latina, Hispanic, Chicano, Mexican American,* and *Cuban American.*
- Take action. For example, parents and students might write the local newspaper to ask about how their community is represented in news photos or in the comics.

ACT TO ENGAGE FAMILIES IN CRITICAL LITERACY INQUIRIES

This is challenging work, isn't it? Some of you may want to engage students in critical literacy inquiries but feel it is too risky; some of you don't see how to work it into a packed mandated curriculum; and some of you may flat out disagree that it's appropriate to teach students from a critical literacy stance. Perhaps the last thing you want to do is invite family involvement in discussion of controversial issues.

But that's exactly the place to start. Critical literacy inquiries address the books, media, and issues that surround children and families. So here are some possible starting points that are already familiar, a critical nudge based on family connections we've already explored:

- During the family visits you plan (see Chapter 3), ask families about issues in the community or their neighborhood that they'd like their children to learn more about.
- When children raise issues in class, ask them to go home and talk with their parents and report back. Start an inquiry with these multiple perspectives in mind.
- Ask your students the questions Maria Sweeney (see above) has her students ask of texts such as, Is this fair? Is this the whole story? Who benefits and who suffers? When students take books home, include these discussion questions in family–school journals for families to discuss.
- If you do a photography project (see Chapter 4), help students generate critical questions of the places they have photographed, write about them, and ask their parents to respond to those questions as well.

Critical literacy discussions, inquiry projects, and action for social change can engage students who seem bored, defeated, or defiant about school. They can engage family members like Denise's mother, who shared her painful story about not being able to give her order at a fast-food window, because they recognize that they are helping their children become readers and writers who can change the world.

READ TO LEARN MORE

Cowhey, M. (2006). *Black ants and buddhists: Thinking critically and teaching differently in the primary grades.* Portland, ME: Stenhouse.

Teacher Mary Cowhey collaborates with students, their families, and community leaders and activists to address the issues that arise in her classroom of highly engaged critical thinkers. Cowhey reflects honestly and in detail about the challenges, organization, and great rewards of working collaboratively for a more just society.

Jennings, L., & O'Keefe, T. (2002). Parents and children inquiring together: Written conversations about social justice. *Language Arts, 79*(5), 404–414.

In Tim O'Keefe's second grade classroom students study the civil rights movement, the internment of Japanese Americans, and other historical events. They take home short passages on these subjects, read with their parents, and have a written conversation about events, opinions, and feelings.

CHAPTER 8

Make the Most of Conferences

Instead of telling parents what was going on in the classroom, I thought of our conferences as a chance to celebrate the successes and identify the areas of growth for the remainder of the academic year. Instead of seeing parents as an audience I needed to perform for, I saw them as a knowledgeable part of a conversation about both curricular and extra-curricular topics. Instead of seeing the student—often brought to the conference—as a nuisance that must be entertained while I spoke with her parent, I relied on her participation in the conversations about her work.... Soon families were attending conferences at a frequency of more than 90%. (Hansen, 2009, p. 3)

CHRIS HANSEN, a second-grade teacher in a Title 1 school serving African American and Latino families, made these profound shifts after becoming increasingly dissatisfied with traditional parent–teacher conferences. He didn't set out to have student-led conferences, but that is where he ended up—the students and their parents showed him the way.

DISCUSS PARENT–TEACHER CONFERENCES AT YOUR SCHOOL

It seems like expectations keep getting added to conferences: going over test scores, explaining new curriculum and district mandates, and asking parents to help "manage" their children through various discipline plans and contracts. Parents often leave frustrated at being talked to for 15 or 20 minutes, and teachers often leave exhausted. And students? Some can't wait to hear what their teacher said about them; others dread the report.

What are conferences like at your school? How do you discuss a student's reading and writing development? You might start with identifying what the key stakeholders—parents, teachers, and students—think about the way conferences are currently conducted. If your school is not interested in a school self-study, find a group of teachers who are—perhaps your grade level, or an invitational study group.

School Self-Study: Faculty Meeting 1

1. Invite every teacher, paraprofessional, administrator, and support staff member to reflect individually by writing for 10–15 minutes on these questions:

    -   What is the current structure of conferences? What really happens during them?
    -   How and when do we discuss a child's literacy learning?
    -   What results do we hope for from parent conferences?
    -   What are we doing well? Who is benefiting?
    -   What are we doing poorly? Who is disadvantaged?

- What would be the ideal conference? Think about time, content, place, relationships, and the role of conferences in student learning.

2. In small groups, discuss each question.

3. Decide how to gather information from students. For example, you might have a morning meeting or other class meeting guided by some of the following questions:

   - What do you think happens during parent–teacher conferences?
   - What would you like your parents or family to know about your learning in school?
   - What would you like them to know about your reading and writing?
   - What would you like your teacher to know about you as a learner, reader, and writer outside of school?
   - What do you think your teacher and family could talk about that would help you learn, at school and outside of school?
   - (If the school already has student-led or student-involved conferences) What is your role during conferences? What works well for you? How do these conferences affect you as a learner? What could we do to make these conferences more effective?

4. Determine how you can gather information from families. For example, students might interview the members of their family with questions such as the following:

   - What are the most important things about parent–teacher conferences to you?
   - What would you like to happen at conferences?
   - Has anything happened at a conference that made you upset?
   - What kind of information could you share at conferences that would help my teacher understand me better as a learner?
   - What do you want to know from my teacher that could help us learn together at home?
   - What do you think my role as a student should be at

conferences? (If you are currently involving students, or are planning to, students might ask several questions related to student involvement.)

School Self-Study: Faculty Meeting 2 or Parent–Teacher Advisory Team Meeting.

SWOT the data—analyze Strengths, Weaknesses, Opportunities, and Threats. Ideally, teachers and parents (and students) would work together analyzing the data (Figure 8.1). First in small groups, then as a whole group, chart the information from faculty and staff, students, and families.

EXPLORE HOW OTHERS HAVE MADE THE MOST OF CONFERENCES

Student-Led, Parent-Involved Conferences: Preparing for the Conference

When each of my children was in second grade, they had the good fortune to have an insightful teacher, Sandy Sanders, who held student-led conferences (SLCs). She prepared the children to present their own work, to go over their accomplishments, and to explain

FIGURE 8.1. SWOT Chart Format with Data Analysis Questions

Strengths	Opportunities
What is currently working well for some or all parties? What do you want to keep?	What ideas have potential? How might such changes affect the relationships among teacher, student, and family member? How might such changes increase student learning?
Weaknesses	**Threats**
What is not working well? Why?	What are the barriers to pursuing the opportunities? How might we overcome these barriers?

areas where they needed further work. These were the best conferences I ever attended. But that was decades ago. Do teachers in today's test-driven, time-crunched schools find student-led conferences valuable?

Jennifer Ellis is a fifth-grade teacher in rural Georgia who swears by student-led conferences:

> It takes the pressure off having a possible situation where the kid, teacher, and parent aren't on the same page because we're all there. The students present their strengths and weaknesses to their parents, and back it up with student work. The parents like that they are having the conversations parents typically want to have with kids at home, but may not get the kids away from the TV long enough to make the conversation meaningful. (Personal communication, July 24, 2008)

Students Prepare to Lead the Conference. Jennifer prepares her students well. Together they develop an agenda for the conference, and students gather the documents that will show parents their learning. Then she does a quick run-through with each student to build their confidence in sharing their work. For example, one student said that she was a good reader because she had read 29 books during the quarter, and her reading log documented this. Jennifer pointed out that these were picture books and that she felt the student was ready to read chapter books; the child then named several authors and series she wanted to read.

A first-grade teacher, Molly Rose, prepares her students similarly because "in learning how to gather the evidence, make informed judgments, and report their self-evaluations to their parents and teacher, they develop the skills of documentation and discernment" (Lawrence-Lightfoot, 2003, p. 91). Molly's students kept portfolios containing their work and self-evaluations, including checklists for reading, writing, math, social studies and personal growth. Early in the year Molly read the items on the checklists to the children in small groups as they looked at their work; by the end of the year, they could read the checklists themselves as they marked M (most of the time), S (some of the time), and N (not yet).

Based on their documentation of several schools that implemented three-way conferences, Davies, Cameron, Politano, and Gregory (1992) suggested several additional ways of preparing students:

- Provide a conference guide sheet that might include Things I'm Really Good At, Two Things I Need to Improve, Things to Show My Learning, and My Goals for Next Term.
- Pair younger students with older ones who are experienced at conferencing to rehearse the conference.
- Work with the class on setting goals. For example, the teacher might ask, "How could we improve our writing?" The class brainstorming might include goals such as "using strategies our favorite authors use," "revising after writing conferences," and "getting better at editing our own pieces."
- To set individual goals, brainstorm with students and ask them to select the ones that are most important. The students then write on their conference guides, "My goal in reading is _____ because _____." Writing their goals helped students present them more confidently.

Parents and Caregivers Prepare to Participate in the Conference. Let families know what to expect and how to prepare, especially if student-led conferences are new to parents. (See online supplementary materials for parents.) In a phone call, e-mail, or letter to families, teachers and/or students can share the process and forms they'll use. The sample letter used by Davies et al. (1992) included this information:

- You and your child will have time to look over his or her collection of work and the classroom displays and learning centers.
- You and your child will then meet with me to discuss your child's strengths and any concerns and set new learning goals for the upcoming term.
- Your child is prepared to take an active part.
- There will be opportunities for you to ask questions, make comments, or express concerns.
- If you have any issues you wish to discuss privately with me following the three-way conference, a sign-up sheet is available. (p. 27)

I would also invite parents to have an active role in the conference adding, for example, "Please bring examples from home that show what your child does as a reader and writer. For example, you might bring correspondence with a family member, a game she especially likes, ways she helps the family such as making grocery lists, or things she reads for fun or related to your family life."

Teachers Prepare to Participate in the Conference. First, talk about who will attend the conference from the school. Include any teacher who has responsibility for a major portion of the child's instruction such as a reading specialist or special education teacher. The student and family members might want to include the media specialist, the art, music, or physical education teacher.

If possible, find a teacher, a parent, and a student who have participated in student-led conferences. Invite them to share a "live" or videotaped conference. There are some delightful student-led conferences on YouTube. Davies et al. (1992) shared additional ways teachers prepared:

- Role-play situations that might concern teachers such as a student who freezes, or a parent who will only address the teacher. They noted, "The staff were careful not to mock anyone through their role-play" (p. 31).
- Brainstorm a T-chart of possible problems and solutions.
- Plan ahead to schedule interpreters (see Chapter 2 for strategies on finding and conversing through interpreters).

What if you can't find an interpreter in time? Miriam McMillan teaches second grade in rural Georgia. Her most interesting student-led conference was conducted almost entirely in Spanish—which she doesn't speak. Miram explained:

Enrique led his conference in Spanish so that his parents could understand everything. I didn't really understand a lot of what he was saying, but because I had helped him prepare for the conference I had a pretty good idea. Every once in a while he would stop and tell me about the goals they were setting. (Personal communication, December 1, 2008)

Student-Led, Parent-Involved Conferences: During the Conference

While they are waiting for their family's conference turn, students can explain writing and other projects displayed on walls outside the classroom. When it's time, the student introduces everyone. Students then show evidence of their learning such as their writing folders with rough and final drafts, a reading response log, or a live demonstration of finding information on the Internet. Next students tell what they have learned or how they have grown, areas that need improvement, and learning goals for the next grading period. The teacher(s) and the family member(s) then bring in any topics they want to discuss further. Parents then share evidence of student learning outside of school. The teacher takes notes, perhaps on a laptop to print out a copy for everyone immediately, although the computer is something of a barrier.

While each person attending the conference may have his or her own notes, the official report is developed together during the conference. Your form might look something like Figure 8.2.

The last part of the conference is crucial for future learning. Family member(s), teacher(s), and the student agree on goals specific to the student's development as a reader, a writer, and so on. Then everyone indicates what he or she is going to do to help meet these goals. I particularly like 11-year-old Sheena's learning plan (Davies et al., 1992). Her goals were: (1) to improve spelling in written work, and (2) to practice estimating measurements. Her plan stated action to be taken by each participant:

- *Student*: I will read over my work and circle the spelling mistakes I find and try to correct them. I really want to get better at using the computer to publish my work.
- *Parent(s)*: We are building a barn, and there will be plenty of opportunities for Sheena to practice estimating and measuring.
- *Teacher*: I will include more informal estimation activities for the whole class and help Sheena develop ways to recognize and correct misspellings. (p. 11)

Student-Led, Parent-Involved Conferences: After the Conference

The most important part of conferences is what happens in the following weeks. Students should leave the conference with the confidence that they have at least two adults who are going to help them learn, that those adults are going to communicate with each other

FIGURE 8.2. Example of Learning Report

Luke's Learning Report

for First Quarter, Third Grade in Ms. Nelson's Class

Our curriculum this quarter included an integrated unit on the environment, "green" jobs, and endangered animals

    Reading: informational texts

    Writing: informational texts

    Math: charts, percentages

Strengths: [*during* the conference, the teacher records the strengths the student presents, and those the teacher and family members add]

Challenges: [*during* the conference, the teacher records the challenges or areas needing improvement the student presents, and those the teacher and family members add]

Learning Plan

Goals:

    Actions to be taken by

        Student:

        Family member(s):

        Teacher(s):

Signatures:

Note. Data in form is author's. Form is adapted from *Together is better: Collaborative assessment, evaluation, and reporting* (p. 11), by A. Davies et al., 1992, Winnipeg, Canada: Portage & Main Press.

---

regularly, and that they believe in the child's ability to learn and will be actively involved in supporting them. Jennifer Ellis noted,

> We're continually monitoring these goals until the next confer-ence. I think the parents become more active simply because their child is right there and expects it. . . . Parents have even

sent me notes and e-mails asking me to talk with their child to remind them about working on their goals at home. (Personal communication, July 24, 2008)

Student-Led, Parent-Involved Individualized Education Plan (IEP) Conferences

While all parent-teacher-student conferences are important, the IEP meeting is arguably the most critical. Students who learn differently are often the most vulnerable, and they and their parents have the greatest need to be actively involved. For a moment, let's put ourselves in the shoes of a parent of a child with special needs (some of us have walked many miles in those shoes). A staff person from the school has asked you to come to something called an IEP meeting. You don't really know what it's all about. What do you do?

Increasingly, parents turn to the Internet for information. Here is the very first thing that came up when I googled "IEP meeting," posted on About.com: Special Needs Children:

Question: Who attends an IEP meeting?

Answer: The IEP meeting is attended by members of the Child Study Team, which usually includes a social worker, a psychologist, a learning specialist, and your child's teachers and therapists. Parents are *always* to be included in IEP meetings. You have a right to be notified in advance and to change the date if necessary. Although IEP meetings are rarely pleasant, do *not* be tempted to skip them. You are the expert on your child, and are therefore the most essential member of the team. (http://specialchildren.about.com/od/specialeducation/f/iepfaq02.htm)

Not very welcoming, is it?

In his counseling with African American parents, educational consultant Jawanza Kunjufu (2002, 2005) recommends strategies for reducing the overrepresentation of African American children in special education. Since difficulties in school-defined reading performance are often central in IEP meetings, it is especially important to foster dialogue and develop partnerships that support students. Kunjufu recommended several strategies to parents attending IEP meetings, including the following:

- Provide a video tape of your son [or daughter] that documents his attention span either reading a book or playing games . . .
- Ask how special education classes are evaluated.
- Ask how soon children are mainstreamed . . . and if they return to the mainstream classroom at grade level.
- Ask, "What can I do to assist you?" and develop a specific plan to review progress (2002, pp. 121–123).

These are difficult questions. What answers would a parent asking such questions at your school receive? Here are some actions you might take to address the issues Kunjufu raised:

1. Research your school's practices. Don't get defensive; get data. Are African American males overrepresented in classes for behavior problems? Are children living in poverty retained more frequently? Do a few teachers account for the majority of referrals or retentions?
2. Use the data to start a schoolwide conversation. Read. Make changes. Address inequities.
3. Hold meetings with small groups of parents at times and places convenient to them to talk about the IEP process, what is at stake, and how they can prepare and take an active role. You might start with their questions and concerns, and end with group-generated suggestions.
4. Ask parents to share their child's learning at the IEP meeting. In addition to taping the child reading or playing a game, parents might photograph projects students initiate at home, collect writing, and document time on the computer and the various literacies involved.
5. Generate possibilities with parents for what they might do at home to support their child's reading and writing development based on student interests. These can be written into the IEP so that it is truly a joint document.
6. Revisit everything we explored about student-led, parent-involved conferences. They are even more important for students who learn differently, who feel like failures, or who have disengaged from school.

These actions take us from compliance to collaboration, from depersonalized objectives to collaborative action plans.

ACT TO MAKE THE MOST OF CONFERENCES

You've gathered and analyzed data from teachers, families, and students. You've read about student-led, parent-involved conferences and given special consideration to IEP conferences. You are ready to make some decisions, so you might start with these questions.

- Who is eager to make changes? They can pilot the idea, collect data, record strategies, and work out the kinks. Put it on the faculty meeting agenda twice a year to monitor effectiveness and invite more teachers in.
- When will you start? Should you give it a try during fall conferences and fine-tune during the remaining ones? Should you explain the idea to students and parents at the first conference and then implement at the next?
- Who is the "point person"—you know, the one who's going to make sure all your good ideas really happen?

READ TO LEARN MORE

Lawrence-Lightfoot, S. (2003). *The essential conversation: What parents and teachers can learn from each other.* New York: Random House.

Lawrence-Lightfoot, a Harvard professor (and parent), interviewed parents and teachers to learn their perspectives on parent–teacher conferences. She pays particular attention to issues of race, class, gender, culture, and language, and offers both thoughtful insight and sound advice.

Davies, A., Cameron, C., Politano, C., & Gregory, C. (1992). *Together is better: Collaborative assessment, evaluation and reporting.* Winnipeg, Canada: Portage & Main Press.

Written for elementary teachers, the book describes teacher–parent–child conferences, informal communication, collecting evidence of learning, and student reflection on their learning. The authors include classroom examples and reproducible forms to prepare for, conduct, and reflect on three-way conferences.

CHAPTER 9

Strengthening Partnerships: What Will We Do Next Year?

Rosario Ordoñez-Jasis interviewed Mexican American parents, often portrayed by schools as uninvolved, about literacy interactions with their children. Gustavo's mother, who had dropped out of high school when he was born, explained that although she worked from 3:30 to midnight, she still helps her son with literacy:

> I try to do as much as I can on the weekends, my days off, and when I drop him off and pick him up from school. In the car we practice spelling words, or I have him read signs on the road. If we're waiting at the

doctor's [office] we read books together, at the market we read labels. I do whatever I can. . . . I don't want him to fall behind. I want him to finish school. (Ortiz & Ordoñez-Jasis, 2005, p. 114)

As we've seen in countless examples, many parents want to do whatever they can to help their children become readers and writers. We've explored many ways teachers and families have created partnerships that support the kind of involvement that Gustavo's mother was eager to do to encourage her son's literacy learning at home (or in the car, or at the market).

WHAT DIFFERENCE HAVE FAMILY–SCHOOL PARTNERSHIPS MADE?

Way back in the introduction, I invited you to engage in dialogue with me and with educators and families. You've learned from families, taught their children, and created new and perhaps enduring relationships. What difference has it made for student learning?

Questions for Reflection

In my classes on family–school partnerships, we start each session with time to write in response to two questions. I think these would be great questions to write about at the beginning of monthly faculty or grade-level meetings:

1. What have I learned from families this week?
2. What difference has it made for my teaching and for students' learning?

The teachers, all rushing in from full days of teaching and some from long drives, came to treasure that time to reflect. In answer to the first question, they wrote things like these:

- Wahab has a talking bird.
- Reynaldo's fifth-grade neighbor Jose is willing to help him learn letter sounds
- Alexander's mom wants to know how to help him at home. He lives next door to his cousin who was in my class last year.

- Shaunti's mom writes poetry and is a chef. Shaunti loves to help her mom in the kitchen.

This knowledge of families came from new family engagement practices. Some visited the homes of every family, some implemented dialogue journals, some focused on student-led, parent-involved conferences. Not everything they learned translated directly into instructional practices, of course—I don't think there was a unit on talking birds.

But very often, the connection made a direct difference for a child's learning. Miriam McMillan learned that Danny was being raised by his grandparents, and was not allowed to spend time alone with his mother. His grandma was very concerned about the emotional effects of the family situation and the effects on his schoolwork, especially reading. After their first visit, Miriam and Grandma decided to exchange a journal every week with ideas to help him become a more confident reader. Miriam often sent ideas in the journal specific to Danny's needs, and Grandma began working with Danny at home.

Jennifer Beaty, who teaches in an urban school with immigrant families from many parts of the world, visited with every family early in the year, despite some concerns about how they would negotiate language issues. Ana's mom said she would like homework translated into Spanish so she could help Ana. Jennifer was able to get this support from the school for some assignments. Several months later after she talked with Ana's mother about how well Ana was doing in school, Jennifer reported:

> She's so proud of her. She was shy last year and didn't tell her mom much about what was going on at school. Now she talks about school every day. Maybe it's because I went to her home and saw her photo album and met with her mom. Maybe because I started getting the homework translated into Spanish. (Personal communication, December 1, 2008)

Not all issues can be resolved so successfully. One family from Ghana spoke Twi. Jennifer could not find a translator or an online translation program so they weren't able to establish written communication. What would you have done?

TABLE 9.1. Family–School Partnerships for Literacy Learning

What did I do?	What did I learn?	What difference did it make?

A Process for Evaluation

So what difference has DEAR—Discussing, Exploring, Acting, and Reading—made for the dears in your classroom? Think about what you were already doing and what you tried in order to create partnerships that supported literacy learning. Prop a class picture in front of you so that you can see each child's face and write as much as you can in each column of Table 9.1. Now turn the paper over. Look at the class photo again. Write honestly and from the heart—who did you miss? Are there students and families you wish you could have connected with? What difference might a close partnership have made for that child as a reader and writer? Discuss your individual charts in whatever group you've been working all year—grade-level teachers, like-minded colleagues, whole faculty, or parent–teacher group.

Next, as a school or smaller group, dig out that chart you made way back in Chapter 1, the three-column Analysis of Current Family Involvement Efforts. What changes have you made? What difference do you feel it has made for literacy learning?

Now you know where you are, what you've accomplished, and you are starting to get a handle on what difference it has made for teachers, students, and families. What's next?

A PLANNING RETREAT TO ADVANCE

Some schools I've worked with have planning retreats, sometimes during postplanning, sometimes during the summer, sometimes for 2 days, and sometimes just for an afternoon. Sometimes it's just the leadership team, sometimes the whole faculty. Sometimes it's at a real "retreat" spot—someone's mountain cabin or comfy living room— and sometimes in the school cafeteria. Where and when you "retreat to advance" will depend on goals, finances, and leadership.

There is one given. This conversation has to include family members.

To find out how our efforts are affecting families, there needs to be continual dialogue among teachers and families, throughout the year and across the years. The curriculum changes, teachers move, administrators retire, neighborhoods change—partnerships must evolve to stay vital.

What will you do at this annual retreat? Here are some suggestions:

1. Bring data. Bring the analyses you did in the previous section. What existing data might inform you, for example, classroom or media center checkouts, writing folders, dialogue journals, or reading assessments? You might even take a peak at test-score patterns. Gather parent feedback on specific practices such as Weekend Journals, family visits, and poetry projects. Parents attending the retreat may gather this information from families in their child's class through informal chats, telephone calls, or neighborhood meetings. Students might interview their parents. Teachers might pose written questions in well-established family–school journals. (See online supplementary materials for parents.)

2. Interpret data. Work in small groups—parents or guardians and teachers together—making sense of the information. Ask questions, make charts, look within and across grade levels, and keep the focus on student learning.

3. Discontinue ineffective practices, refine promising practices, and create new practices. Would anyone die if you didn't have the fall festival? OK, parents are saying it's important to them, the kids love it, and it's a community tradition. Maybe next year you can incorporate a National Public Radio–style StoryCorps booth and create podcasts of family stories. Maybe families can draw and share neighborhood maps at one table. What new practices intrigued you as you discussed ideas in this book? Brainstorm how a photography project, parent-teacher-child writing projects, or must-read text explorations might be meaningful.

4. Figure out the barriers and how you might cross them. Let's say there's a consensus among educators and families

that some kind of weekly dialogue journal focused on learning is your highest priority for next year. How will these differ by grade level, and how will student roles evolve? Who will translate if needed—including in Twi? What can the administration do to support this instructional dialogue (buying journals, providing duty-free lunch to give teachers time to respond, increasing classroom libraries)? What if some families feel this is a burden, or intrusive? What if some teachers are stressed about the time it will take to respond?

5. Share plans with all families, and ask for their input. Plan specifically for inviting all families into partnership relationships and for creating dialogue about the plans that the few have made for the many.

EXTENDING THE DIALOGUE

At the beginning of this book I invited you into a dialogue. I wish I could have listened in on all the conversations around the partnerships you created, how families and teachers came together to support learning, and how children became more engaged readers, writers, thinkers, and citizens in the world. If this is truly a dialogue, then I want to learn from you.

Other teachers want to learn from you as well, so extend the dialogue by studying and writing about your particular partnerships. Publish your experiences in professional journals, school district newsletters, and local newspaper columns. Spark dialogue about partnerships by presenting at local, state, and national professional conferences. Get on the agenda for a local school board meeting. Or just mention in the teacher's workroom, "You know, since Monique, her dad, and I have been corresponding in the Weekend Journal, she has been writing so much more insightfully about different characters' points of view in our author study of Jacqueline Woodson. She asked if she could write during recess today." I can just hear the questions—and the dialogue.

References

Ada, A. (2001). *Gathering the sun: An alphabet in Spanish and English*. New York: HarperCollins.

Ada, A., & Campoy, I. (2004). *Authors in the classroom: A transformative education process*. New York: Allyn & Bacon.

Alexander, C. F. (1980). Black English dialect and the classroom teacher. *The Reading Teacher, 33*(5), 571–577.

Alexander, S. (1990). *My mom can't see me*. New York: Macmillan.

Allen, J. (2007). *Creating welcoming schools: A practical guide to home-school partnerships with diverse families*. New York: Teachers College Press.

Allen, J., Michalove, B., & Shockley, B. (1993). *Engaging children: Community and chaos in the lives of young literacy learners*. Portsmouth, NH: Heinemann.

Allen, J., Fabregas, V., Hankins, K., Hull, G., Labbo, L., Lawson, H., et al. (2002). PhOLKS lore: Learning from photographs, families, and children. *Language Arts, 79*(4), 312–322.

Alim, S. (2007). "The whig party don't exist in my hood": Knowledge, reality, and education in the Hip Hop Nation. In S. Alim & J. Baugh (Eds.), *Talkin Black Talk* (pp. 15–29). New York: Teachers College Press.

Amanti, C. (2005). Beyond a beads and feathers approach. In N. Gonzáles, L. Moll, & C. Amanti (Eds.), *Funds of knowledge: Theorizing practices in households, communities, and classrooms* (pp. 131–142). Mahwah, NJ: Erlbaum.

Ancoña, G. (1994). *El piñatero/the piñata maker*. San Diego: Harcourt Brace.

Angelou, M. (1994). *My painted house, my friendly chicken, and me*. New York: Clarkson Potter.

Barillas, M. (2000). Literacy at home: Honoring parent voices through writing. *The Reading Teacher, 54*(3), 302–308.

Bomer, R., & Bomer, K. (2001). *For a better world: Reading and writing for social action*. Portsmouth, NH: Heinemann.

Cowhey, M. (2006). *Black ants and Buddhists: Thinking critically and teaching differently in the primary grades*. Portland, ME: Stenhouse.

Crews, D. (1996). *Shortcut*. New York: Greenwillow Books.

Crews, D. (1998). *Bigmama's*. New York: Greenwillow Books.

Cronin, D. (2005). *Click, clack, moo*. New York: Scholastic.

Cummins, J. (1989). *Empowering minority students*. Sacramento: California Association for Bilingual Education.

Davies, A., Cameron, C., Politano, C., & Gregory, C. (1992). *Together is better: Collaborative assessment, evaluation and reporting.* Winnipeg, Canada: Portage & Main Press.

Davis, C., & Yang, A. (2005). *Parents and teachers working together.* Turner Falls, MA: Northeast Foundation for Children.

Delgado-Gaitan, C. (2004). *Involving Latino familias in schools: Raising student achievement through home-school partnerships.* Thousand Oaks, CA: Corwin Press.

Delpit, L. (1995). *Other people's children.* New York: New Press.

Dudley-Marling, C. (2009). Home–school literacy connections: The perceptions of African American and immigrant ESL parents in two urban communities. *Teachers College Record, 111*(7), 1713–1752. Retrieved July 7, 2009, from http://www.tcrecord.org/context.asp:contentid=15307

Ewald, W., & Lightfoot, A. (2001). *I wanna take me a picture: Teaching photography and writing.* Boston: Beacon Press.

Fay, K., & Whaley, S. (2004). *Becoming one community: Reading and writing with English language learners.* Portland, MD: Stenhouse.

Fisher, D., & Frey, N. (2008). *Teaching visual literacy using comic books, graphic novels, anime, cartoons, and more to develop comprehension and thinking skills.* New York: Corwin Press.

Frank, C. (2003). Mapping our stories: Teachers' reflections on themselves as writers. *Language Arts, 80*(3), 185–195.

Freire, P. (1970). *Pedagogy of the oppressed* (M.B. Ramos, Trans.). New York: Continuum.

Gibbons, G. (1997). *Click!* New York: Little, Brown.

Giovanni, N. (2008). *Hip hop speaks to children: A celebration of poetry with a beat.* Naperville, IL: Sourcebooks.

Gonzáles, N., Moll, L., & Amanti, C. (Eds.). (2005). *Funds of knowledge: Theorizing practices in households, communities, and classrooms.* Mahwah, NJ: Erlbaum.

Graves, M. (2006). *Teaching individual words: One size does not fit all.* New York: Teachers College Press.

Guggenheim, C. (1995). *The shadow of hate: A history of intolerance in America* [Videotape]. Montgomery, AL: Southern Poverty Law Center.

Hansberry, L. (1971). A raisin in the sun. In L. Patterson (Ed.), *Black theater: A 20th century collection of the work of its best playwrights* (pp. 221–276). New York: Dodd.

Hansen, C. (2009). *Parent-teacher-student academic conferences: A literature review.* Unpublished manuscript.

Henderson, A., & Mapp. K. (2002). *A new wave of evidence: The impact of school, family, and community connections on student achievement.* Austin, TX: Southwest Educational Development Laboratory.

Henderson, A., Mapp, K., Johnson, V., & Davies, D. (2007). *Beyond the bake sale: The essential guide to family–school partnerships.* New York: New Press.

Hensley, M. (2005). Empowering parents of multicultural backgrounds. In

N. Gonzáles, L. Moll, & C. Amanti (Eds.), *Funds of knowledge: Theorizing practices in households, communities, and classrooms* (pp. 143–152). Mahwah, NJ: Erlbaum.

Hesse, K. (1994). *Letters from Rifka*. New York: H. Holt.

Hoffman, M. (1991). *Amazing Grace*. New York: Dial Books.

Hoover-Dempsey, K., Walker, J., & Sandler, H. (2005). Parents' motivation for involvement in their children's education. In E. Patrikakou, R. Weissberg, S. Redding, & H. Walberg (Eds.), *School-family partnerships for children's success* (pp. 40–56). New York: Teachers College Press.

Hubbard, J. (1994). *Shooting back from the reservation: A photographic view of life by Native American youth*. New York: New Press.

Human Rights Campaign Foundation. (2009). *Welcoming schools: An inclusive approach to addressing family diversity, gender stereotyping and name calling in K–5 learning environments*. Washington, DC: Author. Available at http://www.hrc.org/documents/An_Introduction_to_Welcoming_Schools.pdf

Irvine, J. (1990). *Black students and school failure: Policies, practices, and prescriptions*. New York: Praeger.

Jennings, L., & O'Keefe, T. (2002). Parents and children inquiring together: Written conversations about social justice. *Language Arts, 79*(5), 404–414.

Johnson, A. (1989). *Tell me a story, Mama*. New York: Scholastic.

Jones, S. (2006). *Girls, social class, and literacy: What teachers can do to make a difference*. Portsmouth, NH: Heinemann.

Kunjufu, J. (2002). *Black students—middle-class teachers*. Chicago: African American Images.

Kunjufu, J. (2005). *Keeping Black boys out of special education*. Chicago: African American Images.

Lawrence-Lightfoot, S. (2003). *The essential conversation: What parents and teachers can learn from each other*. New York: Random House.

Lewis, B. (1998). *The kids' guide to social action*. Minneapolis, MN: Free Spirit.

Lyon, G. E. (1999). *Where I'm from: Where poems come from*. Spring, TX: Absey.

McCaleb, S. P. (1997). *Building communities of learners: A collaboration among teachers, students, families, and community*. Mahwah, NJ: Erlbaum.

McDowell, J. (2009, March 13–15). How to raise a happy child. *USA Weekend*, p. 24.

McIntyre, E., Kyle, D., Moore, G., Sweazy, R. A., & Greer, S. (2001). Linking home and school through family visits. *Language Arts, 78*(3), 264–272.

McKissack, P. (1997). *Can you imagine?* Katonah, NY: Richard C. Owen.

Mercado, C. (2005). Reflections on the study of households in New York City and Long Island: A different route, a common destination. In N. Gonzáles, L. Moll, & C. Amanti (Eds.), *Funds of knowledge: Theorizing practices in households, communities, and classrooms* (pp. 233–257). Mahwah, NJ: Erlbaum.

Michalove, B. (1999). Circling in: Examining prejudice in history and in ourselves. In J. Allen (Ed.), *Class actions: Teaching for social justice in elementary and middle school* (pp. 21–33). New York: Teachers College Press.

Miller, R. (1991). *Reflections of a black cowboy.* Englewood Cliffs, NJ: Silver Burdett Press.

Morgan, T., & Thaler, S. (1991). *Photography: Take your best shot.* Minneapolis, MN: Lerner.

Moutoussamy-Ashe, J. (1993). *Daddy and me: A photo story of Arthur Ashe and his daughter, Camera.* New York: Knopf.

Neher, A. (2009). *Weekend journals.* Unpublished manuscript.

Nieto, S. (1999). *The light in their eyes: Creating multicultural learning communities.* New York: Teachers College Press.

Ortiz, R., & Ordoñez-Jasis, R. (2005). Leyendo juntos (reading together): New directions for Latino parents' early literacy involvement. *The Reading Teacher, 59*(2), 110–121.

Plemmons, A. (2006). Capturing a community. *Schools: Studies in Education, 3*(1), 83–113.

Rodriguez, R. (1982). *Hunger of memory: The education of Richard Rodriguez.* New York: Bantam.

Shaw, M. (2002). *Ten amazing people and how they changed the world.* Woodstock, VT: Skylight Paths.

Shockley, B., Michalove, B., & Allen, J. (1995). *Engaging families: Connecting home and school literacy communities.* Portsmouth, NH: Heinemann.

Sweeney, M. (1999). Critical literacy in a fourth-grade classroom. In C. Edelsky (Ed.), *Making justice our project: Teachers working toward critical whole language practice* (pp. 96–114). Urbana, IL: National Council of Teachers of English.

Tatum, A. (2005). *Teaching reading to Black adolescent males: Closing the achievement gap.* Portland, ME: Stenhouse.

Taylor, D., & Dorsey-Gaines, C. (1988). *Growing up literate: Learning from inner-city families.* Portsmouth, NH: Heineman.

Taylor, M. (1987). *The friendship.* New York: Dial Books for Young Readers.

TIPS: Teachers Involve Parents in Schoolwork, http://www.csos.jhu.edu/P2000/tips/languagearts.htm

Tizard, J., Schofield, W. N., & Hewison, J. (1982). Collaboration between teachers and parents in assisting children's reading. *British Journal of Educational Psychology, 52*, 1–15.

Willems, M. (2003). *Don't let the pigeon drive the bus.* New York: Hyperion Press.

Wollman-Bonilla, J. (2000). *Family message journals: Teaching writing through family involvement.* Urbana, IL: National Council of Teachers of English.

X, M., & Haley, A. (1965). *The autobiography of Malcolm X.* New York: Grove Press.

Index

About the Author

JoBeth Allen conducts collaborative action research with teachers who are exploring issues of educational equity and social justice. A former elementary school teacher, she is currently a professor in Language and Literacy Education at the University of Georgia, where she and her students explore writing pedagogies, poetry, critical pedagogies, and approaches to research in language and literacy. She also codirects the Red Clay Writing Project (RCWP), a site of the National Writing Project. With RCWP teacher inquiry groups she has studied issues of literacy and social class, and the influence of critical pedagogy on students who risk disenfranchisement by schools. Her books in collaboration with teacher researchers include *Engaging Children: Community and Chaos in the Lives of Young Literacy Learners* (1993) and *Engaging Families: Connecting Home and School Literacy Communities* (1995), both with coauthors Betty Shockley and Barbara Michalove; and *Class Action: Teaching for Social Justice in Elementary and Middle School.* Her best-selling book *Creating Welcoming Schools* highlights partnerships of diverse families and dedicated K–12 teachers that support student learning.